Luis Meléndez Still Lifes

Luis Meléndez
Still Lifes

Peter Cherry
& Juan J. Luna

National Gallery of Ireland
16 June – 5 September 2004

**Published on the occasion
of an exhibition at
The National Gallery of Ireland
16 June – 5 September 2004**

The exhibition is supported by

With the assistance of

ESPAÑA
ACCIÓN
CULTURAL
EXTERIOR

Distributed by the
National Gallery of Ireland

Copyright ©2004
National Gallery of Ireland
and the Authors

ISBN 1904288073

Edited by Susan O'Connor
and Isabella Evangelisti
Design by Jason Ellams
Printed in Belgium by Die Keure

Juan Luna essay translated by
Alison Ribeiro de Menezes
Juan Luna catalogue entries
translated by
Dr Christopher Fitzpatrick

COVER ILLUSTRATION
Luis Meléndez, *Still Life with a
Plate of Cherries, Plums, Cheese
and a Jug* (detail, cat. 2)

FRONTISPIECE
Luis Meléndez, *Still Life with
Apricots and Cherries,* (detail, cat. 19)

ILLUSTRATION PAGE 80
Luis Meléndez, *Still Life with a
Plate of Azeroles, Apples, Pears,
Cheese and Kitchen Utensils,*
(detail, cat. 23)

Acknowledgements

This exhibition is a version of one held at the Museo Nacional del Prado, *Luis Meléndez: Bodegones*, between 17th February–16th May, 2004. We are grateful to Miguel Zugaza, Director of the Museo Nacional del Prado, Gabriele Finaldi, Assistant Director of Conservation and Research at the Museo Nacional del Prado, and Raymond Keaveney, Director of the National Gallery of Ireland, for bringing the exhibition to Dublin. The project could not have been realised without the efficient collaboration of the staff of both galleries. At the Museo Nacional del Prado, we are grateful to Karina Marotta, Head of Exhibitions, Rocío del Casar, Montserrat Sabán, Raquel González and Emilia Cortés. At the National Gallery of Ireland, we are especially grateful to Sergio Benedetti, Keeper and Head Curator, for overseeing all aspects of the exhibition and to Fionnuala Croke, Head of Exhibitions, and Susan O'Connor, Exhibitions Officer, for their proficient management of the project. Isabella Evangelisti also provided indispensable assistance in its final stages. We would also like to thank Bärbel Vosgroene and Jan van Zwam at Die Keure, Belgium and Jason Ellams for producing such a handsome catalogue.

We owe a particular debt of gratitude to HE Enrique Pastor de Gana, Spanish Ambassador to Ireland, for his assistance and enthusiastic support at every stage of the project, and for his help in securing the loan of key pictures. We would also like to thank José André Gallegos del Valle, Deputy Head of Mission and Julio Crespo MacLennan, director of the Instituto Cervantes, Dublin.

This exhibition could not have taken place without the collaboration of the lenders and those persons who have facilitated the loans, for which the organisers are very grateful. In the first place, we are grateful for the extraordinary generosity of the Museo Nacional del Prado for lending twenty of their Meléndez still lifes. As well as those owners who wish to remain anonymous, we wish to thank particularly: Juan Abelló, Plácido Arango, Evaristo Arce, Laura Baeza, Vicente Carranza, Enrique Gutiérrez de Calderón, Derek Johns, William B. Jordan, Rosendo Naseiro, Marilyn Orozco, José María Pi Blasco, Arturo Ramón i Navarro, Conchita Romero, Matías Santos, Domingo Sanz, Anthony Speelman, Juan Várez, José Luis Várez Fisa, Ignacio Martín Salas Valladares, José Antonio de Urbina, George Wachter and Matthias Weniger. We are grateful to our museum colleagues for the provision of loans and for generously sharing information on the works in their charge, and especially wish to thank: the Duke of San Carlos, Juan Carlos de la Mata, Miguel Ángel Crespo and Almudena Pérez de Tudela at the Patrimonio Nacional; Jesús Urrea at the Museo Nacional de Escultura, Valladolid; Emilio Marcos Vallaure at the Museo de Bellas Artes de Asturias; María Margarita Cuyàs at the

Museu Nacional d'Art de Catalunya, Barcelona; Philip Conisbee, Sarah Fisher and Catherine Metzer at the National Gallery of Art, Washington; Timothy Potts, Claire Barry and Patty Decoster at The Kimbell Art Museum, Fort Worth; Keith Christiansen and Charlotte Hale at the Metropolitan Museum of Art; Dawson Carr and Xavier Bray at the National Gallery of Art, London.

Many other colleagues and friends have provided valuable help and information during the preparation of this exhibition, for which we are extremely grateful; Dolores Baltar, Alfonso Campos Olmedo, María Cruz de Carlos, Brendan Dempsey, Emilio Ferré, Consuelo Gallego, Carmen Garrido, José María Madrid, José de la Mano, Christine Meek, Rosemarie Mulcahy, José Luis Nieves Aldrey, Erika Ortiz Rocasolano, Isadora Rose-de Viejo, Alicia Sánchez Ortiz, Natacha Seseña and María Valdés y Ozores.

Peter Cherry
Juan J. Luna

Foreword

Visitors to the Prado cannot fail but be impressed by the marvellous display of canvases by Luis Meléndez, the great eighteenth century still life painter, whose compositions are so prominently on display there. The present exhibition of the artist's work provides an Irish public with the opportunity to view and admire one of the great masters in a discipline which holds such a prominent place in the history of Spanish painting. Within the National Gallery of Ireland's own collection, this tradition is tantalisingly represented, with only a single testimony to the particular genius of Spanish art for such a humble subject matter, through the still life element in Velázquez' *Kitchen maid with the Supper at Emmaus*, which bears revelatory witness to this particular phenomenon. On view in the Millennium Wing galleries are forty pieces by the master, twenty from the Prado, the rest from museums and private collections around the world.

This substantial presentation of master--pieces by Meléndez contribute to a better awareness and understanding of the artist, who was born in Naples to a Spanish family and spent virtually his entire working life in Spain. In examining the extensive array of still lifes on view we are afforded a unique opportunity to consider his extraordinary achievement and assess his development, placing him in his time and highlighting particular aspects of his personality and inspiration, noting his possible encounters, directly or indirectly with other artists.

This exhibition has been organised by the Museo Nacional del Prado and comes to Dublin from Madrid, where it was shown from February to May of this year. We are immensely grateful to the lenders for making their treasures available for this exceptional show, the most important presentation of the master's work outside Spain. The selection was made by Dr. Peter Cherry of Trinity College, Dublin, who co-wrote the accom--panying catalogue together with Dr. Juan José Luna, Curator of Eighteenth Century Painting in the Prado. At the NGI, the coordination of the exhibition was managed by Fionnuala Croke, Head of Exhibitions, assisted by Susan O'Connor and Isabella Evangelisti. The presentation of the exhibits was arranged by Sergio Benedetti, Keeper and Head Curator. Finally, particular thanks must go to HE. Enrique Pastor de Gana who has promoted and supported the project from its inception, realising an ambition to bring about a better understanding and appreciation of Spanish culture among the Irish public; and to José Andrés Gallegos del Valle, Deputy Head of Mission and his staff who worked with Criona Cullen and Orla O'Brien, in the NGI's Development Office, to secure sponsorship for the Dublin show.

Raymond Keaveney
Miguel Zugaza Miranda

Preface

A little over a year ago, when I visited Miguel Zugaza, Director of the National Prado Museum in Madrid, to comment on the Luis Meléndez exhibition that was being mounted at the time for the Prado, I already had in my mind the secret hope that the exhibition could be shown at the National Gallery of Ireland in the future.

My ambition to bring to Dublin this splendid exhibition of the work by such a great Spanish painter has become a reality today. Thanks to the generosity of the Museo Nacional del Prado, its Director, its Deputy Director for Conservation and Research Gabriele Finaldi, the Curators of the Madrid exhibition – old friends Drs. Peter Cherry and Juan José Luna – the Director of the National Gallery of Ireland, Mr. Raymond Keaveney, Sergio Benedetti, Keeper and Head Curator, and so many others in Madrid and Dublin, this exhibition can be open today.

I would like to express the Embassy's gratitude to the Spanish sponsors: *Ferrovial-Cintra*, *Iberia* and *CAF*, whose generous contribution has made this project possible. I would also like to acknowledge the assistance of *España: Acción Cultural Exterior* of the Spanish Ministry of Foreign Affairs.

I am convinced that the exhibition will represent a magnificent discovery for the Irish public. Luis Meléndez – or the so called *pure* still life painter – is the finest example of the Spanish eighteenth century still life painter and one of the leading figures of Spanish painting that century. He had the power of linking the Spanish tradition from the painters of the seventeenth century – such as Zurbarán, Sánchez Cotán and Van der Hamen – to its culmination in the eighteenth century with Goya.

The Irish public, led by the hand of Luis Meléndez who was so close to the objects that he painted, will discover the Spanish gastronomy of the time. Thanks to his exquisite technique, Meléndez had the ability to capture like nobody else, the light shining through the shadows and he rewards our eyes, drenched by this magnificent light, with "every food that the Spanish climate produces". This is how the Prince of Asturias, the future King Charles IV of Spain, described them; he commissioned a series of forty four paintings, many of which are present in the Dublin exhibition.

I very much hope that this exhibition of Luis Meléndez' work, whose value in the world market is constantly increasing, will constitute a true gift for the Irish public and that all those who visit the National Gallery this summer will enjoy contemplating his delicate and beautiful work.

His Excellency Enrique Pastor
Spanish Ambassador to Ireland

Luis Meléndez and the fruits of a frustrated career
Peter Cherry

Still life painting was probably the last thing on the mind of the handsome artist who gazed at himself in a mirror while painting his *Self Portrait* (fig.1). Dressed in a fashionably elegant costume, Luis Meléndez nonchalantly holds in his right hand a chalk holder and with the other offers for the viewer's approbation a folio sheet with a red chalk study of a nude male model, signed and dated 1746. Although Meléndez's fine dress might be considered somewhat impractical for the life class, this draws on a long tradition of painters' self-representations, in which sartorial distinction was an important indicator of the elevated status of their profession. The portrait is also self-advertising in terms of the author's talent; the viewer is asked to admire the proficiency of the young artist in life drawing, to say nothing of his brilliance in conjouring up so convincingly the realistic fiction of the portrait itself and the *trompe l'oeil* drawing.

Meléndez's *Self Portrait*, painted when he was thirty, is the direct product of his personal and professional circumstances at this particular time. Although its first owner is unknown, one of the reasons for its creation was to celebrate Meléndez's situation and prospects in the recently founded Academy of Fine Arts in Madrid. Luis Meléndez's father, Francisco Antonio Meléndez (1682-1752) had petitioned king Philip V (reigned 1700-1746) for the establishment of an academy in 1726. In 1744, the king founded the provisional

Academy under the directorship of the royal sculptor Giovanni Domenico Olivieri, in which Francisco Antonio was made an honourary director of painting.[1] Luis Meléndez was among the first students to be admitted to the new academy and achieved outstanding results in drawing.[2] While it is unclear whether the drawing that Meléndez holds in his *Self Portrait* represents one of his prize-winning drawings, there can be little doubt that the painting was conceived in a celebratory spirit of self-congratulation. The gesture is all the more significant in this particular context, since figure drawing was the core activity of the academic programme of the newly founded institution and

1 For the history of the Academy, Bédat, 1989; Úbeda de los Cobos, 1988, I, pp. 255-395.

2 Tufts, 1985, pp. 9, 208.

therefore implied considerable artistic promise for the future.

At this time, Meléndez's star was rising. Before joining the provisional Academy, between 1738-1744 Meléndez had worked as an assistant to Louis-Michel van Loo, (1707-1771), who had been made royal painter to Philip V on his arrival in Madrid in 1737.[3] The stylistic refinement of Meléndez's *Self Portrait* derives from this experience. Although he merely formed part of a team of artists dedicated to copying van Loo's prototypes of royal portraits for the domestic and overseas markets, the artist at least had a foothold in the palace. Meléndez's membership of the Academy also signified a great deal for his future career. Among the reasons for the foundation of the royal academy of arts had been the need to train a pool of native artists in the grand style of figurative history painting for employment by the Spanish crown, and particularly in the decoration of the Palacio Nuevo, the new royal palace designed by Giovanni Battista Sacchetti that replaced the Alcázar, burned down in 1734. At the time he painted his *Self Portrait*, Meléndez, therefore, would have had his artistic sights set on a distinguished career as a court painter. As will be seen, he clung to this idea throughout his life.

The Academy that was the focus of the aspirations of Luis Meléndez in his *Self Portrait* also came to be a cause of his misfortunes. In December 1747, Francisco Antonio Meléndez quarrelled with Olivieri and circulated a copy of a letter of resignation, in which he characterised the Academy as "a very small organisation for my talents" ("muy pequeña empresa para mis talentos"). This was sparked by a slight to Francisco Antonio's honour by finding his reserved place at academic *juntas* occupied by another, a situation that the director did nothing to rectify. The real reason, however, appears to have been smouldering professional jealousy of Olivieri and resentment that his own initiatives towards the founding of the Academy had received so little credit. In March 1748, Francisco Antonio made his biggest miscalculation by publishing his letter of resignation, denouncing Olivieri and claiming for himself the honour of founding the Academy. He had his son Luis personally deliver this inflammatory material to the Academy. This affront to the authority of the Academy caused Francisco Antonio immediately to be relieved of his teaching post. Luis was formally expelled from the Academy on 15th June 1748.[4]

Meléndez, father and son, were relatively unaffected by this rupture with the Academy in the short term. The mainstay of Francisco Antonio's career was miniature painting, over which the Academy appears to have had little influence at this time. On Francisco Antonio's return from Naples in 1717, where he had been a soldier in the Spanish garrison, he quickly became an important painter of royal portrait miniatures for use as diplomatic gifts.[5] In 1725, he attained the title of *Pintor de miniatura de la casa real* and in his court career may well have profited from the connections and influence of his brother, the royal painter Miguel Jacinto Meléndez (1679-1734).[6] In 1728, Francisco Antonio signed with his royal title an *exvoto* commemorating his family's deliverance from a storm on their return to Spain from Naples over ten years earlier (fig. 2).

3 Luna, 1982.

4 Tufts, 1985, pp. 12-13, 208-213; Bédat, 1989, pp. 44-50.

5 Espinosa Martín, 1989a.

6 Oviedo-Madrid, 1989-1990.

Fig. 2: Francisco Antonio Meléndez,
Exvoto of the Meléndez Family, 1728
Tempera on vellum, 39,2 x 32,3 cm
Madrid, private collection

While a ship is violently tossed on a stormy sea in the background, Francisco Antonio represented himself and his family safely ashore on a Spanish beach, kneeling devoutly in gratitude for the protection of the Virgin of Atocha, through the intercession of St. Charles Borromeo, and the agency of God the Father beyond. Francisco Antonio portrayed himself as an elegantly attired gentleman, holding the hand of his two-year-old son Luis, whom he appears to offer into the protection of the Virgin and for whose life he gives thanks. The child gazes at his father and gestures towards his mother, María Josefa Durazo, holding his newborn sister Ana (1717-1760), while, shown in prayer, is the five-year-old Clara (1712-1734). Painted

at a time when his career was flourishing, Francisco Antonio would appear also to show his devotion and gratitude to the patron of Madrid who had assured his destiny at the Spanish court and to hope for the future success of his son, who was by now a child of twelve years old. Moreover, the *exvoto* hung in the sanctuary of the Virgin of Atocha in Madrid and therefore publicly advertised Francisco Antonio's expertise in painting portrait miniatures. Indeed, he enjoyed a lucrative business in the production of miniature paintings for titles of nobility (*cartas ejecutorias*), as well as miniatures of devotional subjects, in which enterprises his principal assistant became his daughter Ana.[7]

In a grand gesture of disdain for the Academy and assertion of artistic independence, in 1749 at his own expense Francisco Antonio sent his son Luis to Rome to continue his artistic studies. Luis stayed in Italy for four years and was called back to court at the end of 1753 for his expertise in miniature painting. Francisco Antonio had been charged with leading a team of miniaturists to illuminate a new set of choirbooks commissioned by Ferdinand VI (reigned 1746-1759) for the Royal Chapel to replace those lost in the Alcázar fire of 1734.[8] This was the most prestigious commission in the field of miniature painting of the period and Francisco Antonio would have seen here an important opportunity to reintroduce his son Luis into court circles and to help secure him an artistic future as royal miniaturist after his death.

Luis Meléndez had been trained as a painter of miniatures by his father, but his works argueably exceed his father's in technical refinement. Francisco Antonio did

7 M.C. Espinosa Martín in Madrid, Museo del Prado, 2000, pp. 67-86.

8 Junquera, 1965. This team included Luis's brother, José Agustín Meléndez (1721-1798).

Fig. 3: Luis Meléndez, *Fernando III Receiving the Keys of Seville*, 1757, in the Choirbook of the Royal Chapel, volume 56, page 56v
Tempera on vellum, 65 x 42 cm
Madrid, Patrimonio Nacional, Palacio Real

Fig. 4: Luis Meléndez, *Capital Letter 'O' with a Landscape and Fruit* (detail), in the Choirbook of the Royal Chapel, vol. 41, page. 106
Tempera on vellum
Madrid, Patrimonio Nacional, Palacio Real

not live to see his son complete his masterpiece in the series for the Royal Chapel, the large-scale miniature of *Ferdinand III Receiving the Keys to the City of Seville* and its elaborate accompanying figurative ornament (fig. 3). In this depiction of the king's namesaint, Meléndez clearly went out of his way to impress his royal patrons with his grandiloquent treatment of the historical subject and meticulous detail, even if the figures remain relatively stilted and inexpressive. Moreover, he signed the picture with the self-styled title of royal painter. The Meléndez family also illuminated capital letters and in some of those painted by Luis he employed whimsical still life motifs (fig. 4). The royal choirbooks count among the most admired results of artistic patronage of the reign of Ferdinand VI and, after their completion in 1758, Luis Meléndez might reasonably have expected a distinguished career as a court miniaturist. However, despite his outstanding ability, he does not appear to have prospered in this field. In 1760, an Italian traveller, Joseph Baretti, marvelled at Meléndez's illuminations in the choirbooks, but was dismayed to be told by his guide that the artist then lived in poverty and obscurity.[9]

The first of four unsuccessful petitions for royal preferment that Meléndez presented to the King dates from 1759, followed by

9 Tufts, 1985, p. 19 for Baretti's letter from Madrid of 8 October, 1760.

another in the following year that was occasioned by the death of the royal painter Pablo Pernicharo (c.1710-1760), whose post Meléndez sought to occupy.[10] Meléndez pinned his hopes on the ascent to the Spanish throne in 1759 of Charles III (1716-1788) and the expected need for new court painters. Moreover, he had reason to be optimistic, since on his way back to Madrid in 1753, he had been received personally by Charles in Naples, who had reigned there for the previous twenty years as Charles VII of Naples and Sicily. Meléndez later reported that at this audience he had presented the king with three paintings of "the works of his virtuous deeds" ("los trabajos de sus virtuosas tareas"), that were said to have pleased him, and that in his absence he was given the honourary title of his *Pintor de cámara*. These works, unknown today, were probably flattering images of Charles's reign and his recuperation of Naples from Austrian occupation in 1734. They were evidently also tokens in Meléndez's strategy to secure the patronage of this important prospective patron, that appears to have borne positive results. The fact that Meléndez had been born in Naples, where he still had family, would have made an artistic career at the Neopolitan court viable for personal reasons.

Meléndez's petitions took the conventional form of a professional *curriculum vitae* in which he outlined his services and those of his family to the royal family. He made much of the long service of his father Francisco Antonio Meléndez as royal miniaturist to Charles's parents, Philip V and Elizabeth Farnese. He noted his own role as his father's assistant in the painting of royal portrait miniatures and, in his petition of 1760,

he explicitly stated that he wished to be employed "in imitation of his father". Meléndez also mentioned that he worked for six years as assistant in the studio of the royal portraitist van Loo. In emphasising this aspect of his career, Meléndez staked a claim for a share in the production of royal portraits of the new monarch that would inevitably have been in demand at the beginning of his reign.

Meléndez brazenly declared that he was a prize-winning student of the Academy, since 1752 named the Real Academia de San Fernando, and described how he had subsequently gone to Rome to continue his artistic studies at his own expense. In this way, he sought to assure his prospective royal patron of his academic credentials, as well as his self motivation in the pursuit of artistic excellence. Meléndez claimed that he had been "head hunted", in being called back from Italy in 1753 specifically to paint the choirbooks for the Royal Chapel. He also reminded the king of their previous meeting in Naples and the honour bestowed upon him on this occasion.

In his petition of 1760, Meléndez said that he presently found himself without any court post or commission ("sin destino algunos [sic]"), although eager to serve the king in any work of his choosing. He had been more specific in his previous petition of 1759, when he asked to be employed in works in which he could show his talent, such as figurative history paintings in oil and fresco ("en asumptos de mayor luzimiento como son, las Obras de Ystoria à Oleo, y fresco"). Here, Meléndez not only stated his ambition to demonstrate his virtuosity in the traditional "higher" genres of painting, but clearly

10 Tufts, 1985, pp. 21-22, 213-214; Espinosa Martín, 1989b, p. 75.

angled for a share of the decoration of the new Royal Palace that was expected to be apportioned to artists in Madrid at the beginning of the reign of Charles III.

Meléndez's petitions were, however, turned down. The ultimate decision regarding Meléndez's future lay with the king, who was evidently insufficiently impressed by the candidate's resumé. This was probably a consequence of Meléndez's career to date, despite the positive gloss the artist placed on this in his petitions. His openly stated desire to work on ambitious artistic projects for the King was probably designed to head off any anticipated criticisms of his artistic limitations. However, in his petitions, Meléndez was unable to point to a public work of his in a church in Madrid or Italy that could speak of his ability in this respect. While Meléndez's miniatures for the choir--books of the Royal Chapel were works of undoubted prestige in court circles, it is likely too that his identification with this speciality of painting would have counted against him. Perhaps the old-fashioned style of Meléndez's miniatures, that remained indebted to the works of his father, would also have been a negative factor. It would have been evident to his prospective patrons, then, that Meléndez was untried in fresco and large-scale oil painting that was required for the pictorial decoration of the new Royal Palace. He would simply not have been a match for the royal painter Corrado Giaquinto (1703-1766), who was a dominant influence on artistic affairs at court during his years in Spain between 1753-1762 and, at the time of Meléndez's petitions, was painting fresco decorations in the new Royal Palace in an exciting modern idiom of Rococo illusionism.[11]

The rejection of Meléndez's petitions was a further setback to his career. Francisco Antonio Meléndez had died in 1752, but his son does not appear to have been able to capitalise on his position as court miniaturist. While he probably painted miniatures for the private market, portrait miniatures of the new royal family after 1759 were supplied by other specialists.[12] Perhaps the main reason for this was the fact that Meléndez had not been able to secure the patronage of any influential protector at court, who could have chanelled professional opportunities in his direction. It is unlikely, however, that Meléndez still suffered the ill effects of his expulsion from the Real Academia de San Fernando, since it was the King and influential members of his court, rather than the academy, who ultimately controlled patronage and the professional advancement of artists.[13] Indeed, in the centralised artistic establishment of Madrid, the royal academy was directly dependent on the King and his aristocratic ministers, who held the key positions of authority in the new institution. Perhaps because of his age, Meléndez also appears to have missed out on the opportunities provided to younger painters by the royal painter Anton Raphael Mengs (1728-1779), who arrived in Spain in 1761 and became enormously influential in artistic affairs at court.[14] Meléndez's situation was that of an outsider and effectively remained as such for the rest of his career.

In the absence of official patronage, Meléndez would have had to rely on the open market for a living. He probably painted devotional subjects in miniature and in oil, although signed paintings by him in the latter medium are presently unknown.

11 Cioffi in Indianapolis, Indianapolis Museum of Art, 1996, pp. 27-38.

12 Carlo Casanova (c.1720-1772), who had been appointed royal miniaturist in 1750, continued to supply portraits of the royal family, as did Joaquín de Inza (1736-1811) and the Neopolitan specialist Gennaro Boltri (doc. 1756-1788), among others.

13 Symmons, 1988, pp. 59-92 on relations between artists and the monarchy.

14 Mengs was invited to Spain by Charles III and lived at Madrid between 1761-1769 and 1774-1777. He promoted at court the careers of a number of younger artists, most notably Francisco Bayeu (1734-1795) and Mariano Maella (1739-1819) and, on his second visit, Francisco de Goya.

The quality of his earlier *Self Portrait* (fig. 1) demonstrates that Meléndez could with ease have developed a portraiture practice, although, surprisingly, no other portraits by him are known today. It would not appear to be a coincidence that Meléndez's earliest known still life paintings date from 1759 and 1760 (figs 5, 60, cat.1). Traditionally, still lifes were painted by Spanish artists on speculation and were relatively easy to sell. After his dismissal from royal service on completion of the choirbook miniatures, Meléndez therefore evidently considered this an opportune line of work for an independent artist.

The fact that Meléndez's earliest known still life paintings already show the fund--amental characteristics of his mature style suggests that he had already painted pictures of this kind, although these too are unknown today.[15] Indeed, a significant degree of personal interest in still life painting can be assumed on Meléndez's part, since the genre had declined greatly by this time in Spain and it was not seriously practiced by any of his major Spanish contemporaries at court.[16] The arrival in Madrid in 1759 of the Neopolitan still life specialist Mariano Nani (1725-1804), the son of the well-known still life and flower painter Giacomo Nani (1698-1770), may have reawoken Meléndez's interest in the genre (fig. 11). While Nani can be considered an important rival to Meléndez, most of his time was taken up with his work as a painter at the royal porcelain factory of Buen Retiro and, later, in the production of cartoons on hunting themes for the royal Santa Bárbara tapestry manufacture. In fact, during the period 1760-1780, Meléndez was virtually alone as a still life painter in Madrid

Fig. 5: Luis Meléndez, *Still life with Apples, Walnuts, Box of Sweetmeats and Kitchen Utensils*, 1759
Oil on canvas, 37,5 x 50,3 cm
Madrid, Prado Museum, no. 936

and, consequently, appears to have taken advantage of this situation both to create and corner a market for his pictures at court. The large body of work that Meléndez left, currently standing at well over one hundred still lifes, is testimony to this and a unique achievement for a Spanish artist of the eighteenth century, that places him alongside the greatest still life painters of Europe. However, his earliest clients, his prices and the extent of his market for this type of picture in the 1760s remains unclear.

Meléndez's earliest known signed and dated still lifes came to form part of an extensive series that he painted for Charles, Prince of Asturias (1748-1819, fig. 6). Despite his youth, prince Charles was an active patron of the arts. He developed a particular taste for miniature painting and perhaps his admiration for Meléndez's

15 A quartet of fruit still lifes, inscribed on the reverse with initials matching those of Luis Meléndez and the date 1750, has been published as the earliest known works of this type by the artist. Cottino, 2000; Cottino 2003, p. 464. The attribution of these pictures is, however, unconvincing, since so little of their composition and style relates to Meléndez's earliest known still lifes in Spain

16 London, National Gallery, 1995, pp. 146-153.

miniatures in the choirbooks of the Royal Chapel led to the commission of one of his finest figure paintings. In 1768, Meléndez painted the *Holy Family* (fig. 7), that ten years later was described as hanging in the "alcoba" in the prince's quarters in the Royal Palace, and a replica on copper for the prince's portable oratory, today untraced.[17] Meléndez probably conceived of such an exquisite devotional picture for this important patron as an investment in his future, hoping that it would lead to further commissions and revitalise his court career as a miniaturist. Some awkwardness in the relative scale of the figures and their anatomy, concealed beneath voluminous draperies, perhaps reflects the artist's unease

or lack of practice in figurative painting. However, the miniature is otherwise a work of extraordinary technical refinement. Fine gradations of tone in the modelling of the figures are achieved through a meticulous stippling technique, that also gives the high-keyed flesh tints the luminous perfection of marble, and the draperies are painted in pure primary colours, accompanied by mixed hues of considerable subtlety.

Meléndez's signature on the *Holy Family* (fig. 7) identifies the painting as both his own invention and work, and is humbly placed on the shaded understep at the feet of the Virgin. The work is dedicated to God and the Virgin Mary: "Ludov.[S] Menendez inv. et pinxit ad Dei honorem ac Vigin (sic) matris.

Fig. 6: Anton Rafael Mengs,
Carlos IV, Prince of Asturias, c.1760
Oil on canvas, 152 x 110 cm
Madrid, Prado Museum, no. 2188

Fig. 7: Luis Meléndez, *Holy Family*, 1768
Tempera on vellum, 34 x 44 cm
Masaveu collection

17 Espinosa Martín, 1989b, p. 73. Meléndez received the large sum of 15.000 *reales* for this miniature. He had received 9.000 *reales* for his miniature of *Ferdinand III Receiving the Keys of Seville*.

ann. 1768". A similar dedication of his work to God can be found on one of Meléndez's still life paintings, *Still Life with Partridge, Condiments and Kitchen Utensils* (fig. 16). This qualifier of Meléndez as inventor is particularly meaningful in the context of miniature painting, since this was a speciality much given to the production of copies of other images. In identifying this miniature as his own original invention, therefore, Meléndez claimed that this work, despite its small size, had an equivalent status in creative terms to those on a larger scale and in other mediums. Although parallels are sometimes drawn between Meléndez's miniatures and his eye for detail in his still life paintings, the distance between these two sides of his art can be measured in terms of the different conventions of each. Apart from the intrinsic technical differences between paintings in tempera on vellum and oil on canvas, Meléndez's miniatures are small paintings of lofty themes, that are painted in the grand, idealizing manner of history painting (fig. 3). Even Meléndez's playful vegetable ornament in the borders and capital letters of the choirbooks for the Royal Chapel are imaginary and highly stylised, and betray little, if any, of the close observation of reality that was expected in still life painting.

In 1771, Meléndez won a commission from the Prince of Asturias for an extensive series of still life paintings to decorate his cabinet of natural history, that was the central project of the artist's later career.[18] On 6th January of this year, Meléndez received an impromtu summons to the Royal Palace from María Luisa, Princess of Asturias and was ordered to bring with him all of the still lifes he had in hand, both finished and unfinished. The date of the audience, the Epiphany or feast day of the Kings, may be significant, if the princess considered Meléndez's paintings as a gift to her consort. The documentation notes that the prince already had in his quarters some four or five of Meléndez's still lifes, showing that he both knew and admired his works of this type. During this audience with the royal couple, an agreement was formalised with Meléndez to embark upon an extensive series of still lifes for the prince's cabinet of natural history, a private museum that he had established in his quarters in the Royal Palace. It appears that the numbers of paintings required for the series was at the discretion of the artist. By January of the following year, Meléndez had delivered a total of thirty seven (or forty one) still life paintings to his patrons, the discrepancy caused by the artist's own faulty recollection of the number of pictures supplied. Although some of these may have been earlier paintings Meléndez had in hand, the majority appear to have been recently painted. By January 1772, then, Meléndez appears to have delivered most of the pictures that eventually came to make up the series of forty four paintings.

It is evident from the sources concerning this commission that, although Meléndez was well-paid for his paintings, he sought from the Prince a more permanent form of royal favour.[19] He asked for a lifelong pension in order to secure his long-term services on the project and for any others that might present themselves in the future; as he himself put it, this was to avoid his having to grub a living selling his paintings on the open market. At Christmas 1776, however,

18 Espinosa Martín, 1989b; Tomlinson, 1989. The New Cabinet of Natural History referred to in the documentation for Meléndez's still life paintings, has previously been confused with the Royal Cabinet of Natural History on the calle de Alcalá, that was opened in 1776. The forty-four paintings that came to make up the royal series, whose dated works range from 1759 to 1774, are now divided between the Prado Museum (39), Patrimonio Nacional (4) and the Museo Nacional de Escultura (1).

19 Meléndez priced his still lifes for the Prince by size, at 1500, 3000 and 4200 *reales* for the smallest size, second size and largest sized pictures respectively. These relatively high prices are important indicators of the value the artist attached to his works in this genre.

the Prince cancelled the project. A document concerning the settlement of Meléndez's account of two years later mentions that the painter refused to accept this and submitted written petitions to the Prince, now unknown, demanding an explanation for the decision and treated rudely royal officials who attempted to clarify payments for the works delivered. The same source refers to the artist's high opinion of his own worth and his still life paintings for this project, "el alto concepto q[u]e tiene Menendez de su merito y el de su obra". Indeed, Meléndez's pride, that seems to have been a family trait and is so eloquently expressed in his early *Self Portrait* (fig. 1), would appear to have made him temperamentally unsuitable as a court artist.

Meléndez had evidently conceived of the project as a vast series of still lifes illustrating the natural history of Spain, that had been prematurely curtailed by his patron. In another petition for the post of royal painter that Meléndez made at this time, discussed below, Meléndez described the series in encyclopaedic terms as a representation of "las cuatro Estaciones del año, y más propiamente los quatro Elementos, a fin de componer un divertido Gavinete con toda la especie de comestibles que el clima Español produce en dichos quatro Elementos". By invoking the enlightened spirit of scientific inquiry of his age, Meléndez cast himself as a serious modern artist and appealed to the intellectual interests of his patron. The Prince of Asturias was an enthusiastic amateur of natural history, as was his brother the Infante Gabriel (1752-1785) and other members of the royal family, most notably his uncle the Infante Don Luis

(1727-1785). In their natural history studies, the Prince and his brother were advised by the Augustinian naturalist Enrique Flórez (1702-1773), who probably also guided the Prince in his purchase of the latest international works on natural history, many with fine illustrations.

Still life paintings, in principle, could be considered appropriate decoration for a natural history museum; the fruits, vegetables and animals the pictures represented were products of the natural world, while the pottery, containers, utensils and other objects in them could be considered human artefacts of anthropological interest. Even Meléndez's still life paintings them--selves could have been considered in the latter terms, as products of artistic ingenuity that transformed natural materials of canvas and paint into objects of high cultural value. Meléndez's descriptive painting style, in which things are represented with great accuracy, would also have recommended his pictures as worthy components of a museum devoted to the study of the natural world. While it is difficult to see a clear program--matic rationale to Meléndez's incomplete series, the forty-four paintings of fruits, meat, gamebirds and fish do express something of the range and variety of edible riches of the Spanish peninsula produced in the different Seasons and Elements. For this reason, it would, perhaps, be to err too far on the side of cynicism to think that Meléndez was merely an opportunist who took advantage of the intellectual fashions of his time and the Prince's interest in natural history to promote his still life paintings in this novel way.

On the other hand, the plausibility of the pseudo-scientific dimension to Meléndez's still lifes might well be called into question before the pictures themselves. In a number of these, there is a marked contrast between the stated lofty aims of the artist and the lowly subject matter of the paintings themselves (cat. 12). Nor can these easily be categorised as natural history illustrations. A well-known precedent for botanical still life paintings were the "portraits" of fruits from the Tuscan gardens of the Grand Duke Cosimo III de Medici (1642-1723) by the Italian still life painter Bartolomeo Bimbi (1648-1730), that systematically itemise a comprehensive range of varieties of fruits.[20] However, there was no real equivalent in the tradition of seventeenth century Spanish still life painting to which Meléndez attended for these works in which art and science were so closely related. The Mallorcan artist Cristóbal de Vilella (1742-1803) was employed by the Prince of Asturias from 1772 as taxidermist and illustrator for his cabinet of natural history.[21] Significantly, his pictures of Mallorcan flora and fauna for the Prince follow the conventions of scientific illustration; images of fruits, for example, are anatomised and accompanied by details of their flowers and reproductive parts.

Meléndez's paintings for the Prince of Asturias conform to the conventions of still life painting, rather than natural history illustration. There is little difference in terms of content and presentation between these still lifes and those Meléndez painted for other private clients, as can be seen by comparing kitchen still lifes from the royal series (cat. 12) with those with a different provenance (cat. 13). Indeed, the evidently

tenuous nature of the link between the still life paintings and their ostensible rationale as studies of the natural history of Spain may have been among the reasons for the prince's cancellation of the project in 1776. This would also seem to be confirmed by the fact that by 1778 the entire series had been transferred to the Casita del Príncipe at El Escorial, where the component pictures assumed a more conventional role as decoration of a rural villa.

Encouraged by the patronage of the Prince of Asturias, however, Meléndez considered this an auspicious time to solicit King Charles III once again for the post of royal painter. He submitted a petition in the autumn of 1771, that was resolved against him in August of the following year.[22] Meléndez's account of his merits in this petition essentially repeated those he had submitted over ten years earlier. However, on this occasion he was able to cite his series of paintings illustrating the natural produce of Spain as a demonstration of his abilities in oil painting, as has already been noted. In the document, Meléndez did not refer directly to his pictures as still life paintings, either because his work was so well known at court or because he did not wish to detract from the elevated pseudo-scientific seriousness of his project by awakening prevailing prejudices against the lowly nature of the genre that was its vehicle. Although at the time of this petition, Meléndez was in receipt of payments from the Prince for the series, in a clever manipulation of ideas designed to appeal to the compassion of the King, he claimed that he did not have the means to continue painting the foodstuffs in his pictures, nor even to feed himself. Despite this, his petition

20 Washington, National Gallery of Art, 2002.

21 Azcárate Luxán, 1987; Azcárate Luxán, 1990.

22 Tufts, 1985, pp. 22, 214-216. While Tufts considered Meléndez's petition to date from 1772, in October 1771 the King referred this to the Duke of Losada to deal with as he saw fit.

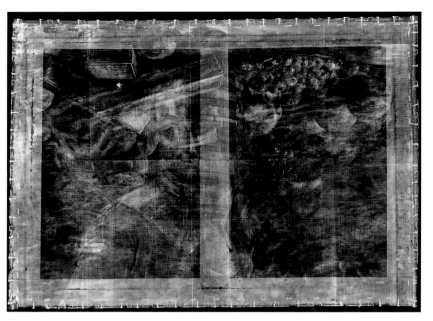

Fig. 8: Luis Meléndez, *Still Life with Oranges, Walnuts and Boxes of Sweetmeats* (x-ray of inverted cat. 34)

23 Espinosa Martín, 1989b, pp. 67-68.

24 The type of canvas on which the portrait is painted appears to be the one Meléndez habitually used. The lack of cusping at the lower edge of the canvas, on which the portrait was painted, suggests that this was cut down here. Technical examination of Meléndez's still life paintings undertaken to date has revealed some reuse of his own canvases, but no demonstrable cases of reuse of painted canvases of other artists. Garrido and Cherry (in print).

25 Rincón García, 1988. The order was instituted on 24 October, 1771 and was approved by papal bull in Rome on 21 February, 1772.

with still life painting by this time may have only compounded his perceived lack of versatility in the large-scale figurative painting needed of royal painters at this time.

Meléndez's professional circumstances at this time may help to explain his decision to paint a new portrait of King Charles III. Technical examination by x-radiograph photography of *Still Life with Oranges, Walnuts and Boxes of Sweetmeats*, signed and dated 1772 (cat. 34), has revealed a finished bust-length portrait of the King beneath the still life, that can be assumed to have been painted by Meléndez himself (fig. 8).[24] The choice of a wide format and the existence of folds of cloth painted at the right of the image suggest that the portrait was originally a three-quarter length, that was subsequently cut down by Meléndez to construct the size of canvas on which the still life was painted. Meléndez appears to have based his portrait on the prototype by Anton Raphael Mengs of 1761, that became the official likeness of Charles III and was much copied (fig. 9). An important aspect of the royal iconography established by Mengs was the smiling face of the monarch, and Meléndez evidently followed. In Meléndez's painting, however, the King was shown in formal dress and wearing a wide sash. The latter is likely to represent the blue and white sash of the Royal Order of Charles III that was instituted in October 1771, although further technical analysis would be required to specify its original colour.[25] At this time, therefore, Meléndez may have decided to paint the King in an updated version of Mengs's prototype in order to celebrate the institution of the new order, as a number of other artists also did. It is possible too that

was finally turned down in the summer of 1772, on the grounds that there was already a full complement of salaried royal painters.

Despite this setback, Meléndez's ambition to become royal painter had not entirely ebbed away. On the death of the royal painter Juan Bautista de la Peña (c.1710-1773) at the end of 1773, Meléndez once again lost no time in soliciting the vacant position and salary.[23] Meléndez repeated his petition of 1771, with the addition of supporting documents, but this was, once again, turned down on bureaucratic grounds of financial expediency. It is likely that the reasons for Meléndez's rejection on this occasion remained the same as they were ten years earlier. In the intervening years, the most significant development in his career had been his specialisation in still life painting. It is likely that this, however, told against him in his latest petitions; Meléndez's identification it was in some way related to Meléndez's petition for the post of royal painter at this time; perhaps he hoped to present the portrait to Charles, or to another influential member of the court, in support of his application, in a repeat performance of his gift of paintings to the King in Naples in 1753. The fact that the image was never delivered and that the artist cut the canvas down, turned the portrait upside down and painted over it one of his most accomplished still lifes may constitute a bitter acknowledgement of his rejected petition and acceptance of the future direction of his artistic career. Such a fit of pique, moreover, would be entirely consistent with what is known of Meléndez's proud personality.

Fig. 9: Anton Rafael Mengs, *Carlos III*, c.1761
Oil on canvas, 154 x 110 cm
Madrid, Prado Museum, no. 2200

The fundamental characteristics of Meléndez's still life painting are already in place in his earliest known paintings of both a horizontal and vertical format dating from 1759-1760 (cat. 1; figs 5, 60). It remains unclear how Meléndez arrived at this point. As is evident from the paintings in this exhibition, however, Meléndez's artistic interests remained relatively uniform for the rest of his career, a fact that makes it difficult to date individual works with any real degree of certainty. Meléndez explored a relatively limited repertoire of conceptual, formal and technical resources in his still life paintings; rather than experimenting in still life, Meléndez chose to perfect the aesthetic characteristics of his art that make his work so distinctive. In short, Meléndez knew his artistic capital and continued to trade on this throughout his career.

Meléndez revived a number of traditional features of Spanish still life painting and exploited these to great effect, as is discussed in the following essay. Much of his still life repertoire is traditional and comprises fruit, comestibles and everyday, utilitarian objects from the kitchen. In his still lifes, as in most earlier pictures of this type, objects are depicted on a table top from a relatively low viewpoint and at close range. Generally speaking, these are represented against a dark background, that, through force of contrast, makes the luminous still life objects register more strongly in terms of their illusionistic volume and chromatic intensity. The use of lighter nondescript backgrounds of a neutral earth tone appears to be a feature that Meléndez developed in his later still lifes (for example cats 9, 15). *Still Life with Figs, Bread and Wine* (cat. 3) appears to have been

Fig. 10: Luis Meléndez, *Still Life with a Plate of Pears and Morello Cherries*
Oil on canvas, 41 x 62 cm
Madrid, Prado Museum, no. 921

the objects it supports. Its "woodenness" is expressed not only in the carefully painted grain and strategically placed knots of the wood, but in Meléndez's exaggerated interest in its worn, distressed surface, with its studied nicks and dents. In all of these paintings, the table is depicted flush with the picture plane and in only a few later works does the artist show its corner or leg (cats 35, 38; fig. 10). In a number of pictures, the objects are composed within the pictorial space demarcated by the front edge of the table (for example, cats 1, 8, 9, 15, 24, 36), although in most works objects slightly overlap this. The front edge of the table has an important illusionistic function in pictures where the latter occurs; since the table edge effectively describes the picture plane, an illusion of continuity between the fictive space of the picture and the real space occupied by the viewer is conveyed by foreshortened objects depicted on the tabletop that appear to project beyond its front edge. This was also an old pictorial device in still life painting (and indeed portraiture), although one that Meléndez used sparingly and with considerable subtlety.

The alternative still life type that Meléndez employed depicts objects in a landscape setting, that he derived from Italian painting (cats 27-31). *Still Life with Fruit, Bread and Wine in a Landscape* (fig. 66) is a particularly ambitious work of this type and is also Meléndez's largest known still-life painting. Despite the open-air setting of these paintings, they depict a similar repertoire of still life objects to those set in interiors and the same means of staging these prevails. The falling landscape feature in these works is little more than a backdrop to an arrangement of still life objects on a

repainted by the artist and its original dark background has been lightened, perhaps in accordance with this evolving aesthetic. In some paintings, the directed lightfall from the left is variable and more atmospheric, and illuminates more strongly the right-hand side of the background (for example, cats 12, 13, 15, 39). This creates tonal counterpoint in which the strongly lit left-hand parts of forms are seen against the darkest area of the background and the shaded right-hand parts of forms against the lighter area of the background. This too was a long-established convention in still life (and other genres of painting), that was designed to increase the illusion of relief in the depicted objects.

The majority of Meléndez's known still lifes represent objects on a wooden table top. In contrast to most earlier Spanish painters, Meléndez, however, pays as much attention to the material details of this surface as piece of flat, bare earth, that is reminiscent of the table top, and lit laterally in the habitual manner of Meléndez's interior paintings. In some pictures, a raised shelf in the landscape feature afforded Meléndez a split-level composition (cats 28, 29, 31). A picturesque ragged ledge at the front of the picture accommodates the low viewpoint by encouraging viewers to imagine themselves placed on a lower plane to the depicted landscape. In some pictures, this too serves an analagous illusionistic purpose to the table edge in his still lifes, as can be seen by the knife handle that projects beyond the landscape ledge in the aforementioned painting in New York.

Meléndez abides by the conventions of still life painting in the choice of a low, close viewpoint, that developed in response to the normative practices of figure paintings. In some pictures the objects occupy almost the entire pictorial field (cats 8, 14, 20) and in others these are cropped to a lesser or greater degree by the vertical sides of the frame (cats 5, 7, 12, 34, 37), both means by which the artist conveys the impression of having homed in on objects to observe them closely. This accepted pictorial practice, of course, differs considerably from viewers' everyday experience of comestibles and kitchen utensils, that are usually seen on tabletops from a higher point of view and a greater distance. This is to say nothing of the lingering gaze of the artist on utilitarian objects that were of absolutely no aesthetic consequence in themselves.

The looming monumentality of objects afforded by the relatively low, close viewpoint in Meléndez's still lifes is emphasised by his handling of perspective. Generally speaking, objects are drawn from an ideal central viewpoint at a height in the upper third of the canvas. In a number of paintings, the foreshortened elipses of tall objects endow these with a dramatic, towering presence, as with the barrel and largest terracotta jug in *Still Life with Oranges, Walnuts and Boxes of Sweetmeats* (cat. 34), the copper cauldron in *Still Life with Salmon, Lemon and Kitchen Utensils* (cat. 36) and the earthenware jugs in *Still Life with Bread, Bottle and Jug* (cat. 9). In a number of paintings in this exhibition, occasional lapses in Meléndez's drawing can be seen in discontinuous elipses that are interrupted by forms in front of them; for example, the elipses of the bowls and plates in *Still Life with Cucumbers, Tomatoes and Kitchen Utensils* (cat. 15), and the silver salvers in *Still Life with Limes, Box of Jelly, Butterfly and Kitchen Utensils* (cat. 24). This ambiguity is more likely to be a consequence of Meléndez's technique and of painting the elipses separately on either side of the form in front of them, rather than an optical effect derived from close empirical observation, since in other pictures a real attempt has been made to draw "correctly" such passages (cats 12, 26, 35, 38, 40).

It is evident from Meléndez's still lifes that perspective is not only used for academic reasons of spatial coherence, but also to dramatise the role of objects in compositions. Meléndez's artifice can be seen in objects that have been deliberately propped up in actual arrangements to allow these to be represented in daring foreshortening, including loaves of bread (cat. 9) and a bronze cauldron (cat. 38). Sharply foreshortened items of cutlery in some pictures act as pseudo-orthogonals that articulate pictorial

Fig. 11: Mariano Nani, *Still Life with Fruit, Sheep, Wild Fowl and a Cat*, 1764
Oil on canvas, 140 x 110 cm
Madrid, Real Academia de Bellas Artes de San Fernando

A defining aesthetic quality of Meléndez's still life painting is his approach to composition, that is sometimes described as "archetectonic". The seriousness with which Meléndez addressed the value of composition in his still lifes parallels that of figurative painting in the grand manner. Indeed, in Meléndez's compositions the objects assume pictorial roles that belie their existence in real life and are more like protagonists of immobile visual dramas. His unusualness in this respect is clear from a comparison with the still lifes of his contemporaries, whose compositions appear more haphazard (fig. 11). Meléndez drew on a tradition of design in the best Spanish still life paintings of the previous century. However, he also possessed a unique ability to orchestrate the objects in his still life paintings into subtle and compelling compositions. Indeed, the repetition of many of the same types of objects in his pictures can be partly explained by their importance as building blocks in these compositions. The changes that the artist frequently made to compositions reflect his uncompromising approach in this respect and some of these are noted in the following catalogue entries. Technical examination of Meléndez's paintings and, sometimes, close scrutiny with the naked eye, shows that the artist was capable of making radical revisions to his compositions as he painted, changing objects and the positions of objects in a significant number of works. More commonly, Meléndez changed the shape and size of objects by adjusting their contours, in order to calibrate precise proportional and formal relationships between them. Significantly, Meléndez generally made such changes on the canvas itself, rather than to

depth (cats 3, 9). The knives painted in a number of Meléndez's still lifes (cats 3, 9) metaphorically "cut through" pictorial space. In two pictures in the exhibition (cats 6, 7), oblong boxes of sweetmeats are arranged in studied disarray and thrust outwards from a central point in wanton perspective. These bear Meléndez's signature, illusionis--tically painted as if scorched into the wood, as does the box that overlaps the table edge in the larger related picture from 1772 in London (cat. 34). The incorporation of Meléndez's signature into the fiction of the still life in this way is a telling expression of his self-identification with the illusionistic power of his art.

any actual arrangement of objects before him, for reasons of pictorial necessity and for optimum compositional harmony.

Meléndez's acute visual awareness of the shape and dimensions of the main objects in his pictures has, with reason, sometimes been described in pseudo-geometric terms. This partly accounts for the strong formal presence of objects in Meléndez's compositions, that is emphasised by his studied modulation of light and shade in modelling the forms. More importantly, however, this faculty allowed Meléndez to compose pictures of great structural lucidity, even when all of the objects depicted in the pictures were not actually before him at any one time. In this way, formal and spatial relationships between the main elements are boldly and clearly stated in his still lifes. Meléndez's grasp of the essential formal character of the objects he painted, be they natural or man-made, also allowed him to see eloquent pictorial possibilities in their relationships and to produce endless variations on given compositional themes. Indeed, the aesthetic

satisfactions deriving from the almost abstract interplay of objects of different shapes and dimensions in Meléndez's still lifes is one of the most distinctive and compelling features of his work. It is also one of the features of his works that appeals so strongly to the sensibilities of contemporary viewers, whose vision of still life has been conditioned by the achievements of modern painting (figs 12, 13).

Meléndez's compositions generally follow a logical pattern; the foreground is usually reserved for the smallest objects, with larger ones occupying the deeper planes of the picture and large, tall and sometimes raised objects in the background, giving an effect of inverse perspective. Meléndez often prioritises the centre of his compositions in chromatic terms, reserving for this area the most strongly illuminated or coloured forms. The studied relations of differently shaped and sized objects cannot be reduced to a formula, however, and depend much on the artist's visual intuition. A number of Meléndez's boldest compositions, for

Fig. 12: Georges Braque, *Basket of Fruit*, 1909
Oil on canvas, 54 x 65 cm
Stockholm, Modern Museum

Fig. 13: Giorgio Morandi, *Still Life*, 1946
Oil on canvas, 37.5 x 45.7 cm
London, Tate Gallery

instance, reverse his habitual compositional procedures and allow large forms to dominate the foreground (cats 8, 13). Wine coolers, funnels and differently shaped bottles provide vertical accents in the deeper planes of the compositions. Large, voluminous objects, such as melons, baskets, wine coolers, barrels, ceramic jugs and metal vessels usually occupy the backgrounds of pictures. In many still lifes, the density of the masses increases towards the background, effectively stopping the eye at this plane and closing off the distance. This is also the function of the falling landscape feature in still lifes set in the open air. Some of Meléndez's most beautiful paintings, however, depict relatively few objects (cats 9, 26, 36), in whose compositions a subtle balance between masses and voids is achieved. The very spareness of these works has the desired effect of concentrating viewers' attention all the more intently upon Meléndez's representational virtuosity in the few depicted objects.

The evidence of technical examination suggests that Meléndez conceived his still lifes in terms of the relations between the primary forms, that were probably arranged in reality in front of the artist, and painted these from the foreground towards the background. As the painting progressed, Meléndez would supplement the composition with secondary forms. Some of these could be extrapolated from the things actually before him, such as partly seen fruits that give a sense of plenitude to the arrangements. Other discrete elements, such as partly seen bowls and jugs, that often appear in the deeper planes of pictures, could be studied from individual objects or from other pictures and inserted into the relevant place in the

still life in hand. Meléndez often added at a late stage in the painting's development individual elements in the very foreground of the composition for reasons of formal and chromatic balance, such as pieces of fruit, garlic cloves, nuts and packets of spices.

Pictorial space in Meléndez's still lifes is generally articulated by the relative position of the objects on the tabletop. The tabletop itself is not projected as a measurable space in the pictures and the absence of perspectival clues in its lateral edges makes its width difficult to gauge. In only a few of Meléndez's known paintings, dating from the later years of his career, is there a glimpse of the extremeties of the table (cats 34, 38; fig. 10). Meléndez usually established the front edge of the table from the beginning of the painting and painted the table in around the objects as the still life progressed, adding in the grain, nicks and dents towards the end of the process. The horizon line of the back edge of the table was sometimes also established from the outset, but was often adjusted as the painting was brought along to accommodate more convincingly the still life objects on its surface. This practice suggests that its dimensions were elastic and responsive to the compositional requirements of particular pictures. The use of broadly consistent linear perspective in the drawing of the objects gives the impression of spatial coherence in the pictures and the modelling of these in light and shade suggests that they have real volume and mass, and occupy particular positions in space. In most paintings, a staged, zig-zag recession into pictorial depth is marked by strategically placed and asymmetrically counterbalanced objects that occupy different planes in the picture.

Meléndez's vertical format still lifes are among his most accomplished and distinctive paintings. These are painted on canvases of the same size as his smallest sized horizontal format works, only turned on their end. Nevertheless, the narrow confines of the vertical field made this a particularly challenging format in which to compose the life-sized still life objects. As can be seen by the consummate works of this type in this exhibition, Meléndez rose to the challenge. He compensated for a lack of lateral extension with an emphatic sense of fictive spatial recession, that is articulated by the relative positions of the counter-balancing objects that mark the different planes of pictorial depth. In many of the works of this type, the objects are accommodated in the narrow field by having been pushed together into close physical proximity to one another, with one form overlapping another, and are seen in increasingly fragmentary form towards the background of the picture (cats 3, 8, 12, 13). The compression of lateral space also lends these a concentrated plastic power, that is particularly effective in dense arrangements of objects that almost fill the entire visual field (cats 5, 6, 10). In some of these, the vertical sides of the frame appear to close in on the elements and squeeze these outwards towards the viewer (cats 8, 12, 13).

It is evident from Meléndez's paintings that he took very seriously the traditional challenge of still life painting as the "imitation of nature". Theoretical discourse interpreted still life painting as a straight-forward copy of an actual arrangement of inanimate objects, whose success was measured by the technical skill of the artist in making the representation of these things as close as possible to their appearance in reality. The artistic lore that supported this oversimplified concept of still life dated from classical antiquity; indeed, one of the best known *topoi* concerning still life as a proxy of nature concerned the painted grapes of the ancient Greek artist Zeuxis, that were so realistic as to deceive birds into trying to eat them. However, the high degree of naturalism that was the strength of still life also condemned it to a lowly status in the academic hierarchy of types of painting.

In Spain, as elsewhere, large-scale figurative religious pictures, such as altarpieces, or fresco paintings were the traditional measure of artistic prowess. Meléndez himself acknowledged this in his petition for the title of royal painter of 1759, when he ambitiously sought the King's patronage for works in which he could best demonstrate his abilities, citing specifically history paintings in oil and fresco. Moreover, the Real Academia de Bellas Artes de San Fernando institutionalised the model of painting as an intellectual art, with its source in the creative imagination of the artist and with drawing as the fundamental means of creative expression. At the core of its curriculum was the systematic study of the human figure as the most noble and challenging subject matter of art, as can be seen in Meléndez's early *Self Portrait* (fig. 1). The neo-platonic artistic theory of beauty that underpinned academic discourse and practice in Meléndez's lifetime defined the duty of the artist to represent idealised forms, by "improving" on nature, rather than merely "imitating" it, in which process exemplary guidance was available in the sculpture of classical antiquity and the figurative art of the Italian Renaissance. In academic terms, the most elevated type of imagery were figurative historical subjects, that expressed an edifying moral and were painted in an ideal style.

It would appear, then, that the period was not propitious to still life painting. However, still life was acknowledged as a legitimate branch of painting, albeit a lowly one. Meléndez would probably have been galled to learn of the Madrid Academy's award of the title of *Académico de mérito* in still life painting to Mariano Nani in 1764. Nani's academic reception piece (fig. 11) is a large and ambitious demonstration of his ability in painting realistically a wide range of subject matters, comprising live and dead animals, fruit, flowers and kitchen utensils. Indeed, Nani went on to specialise in game still lifes and his excellence in the depiction of the fur and feathers of animals made him a preferred artist of the Prince of Austrias in the 1780s. However, still life painting was theoretically excluded from the highest ranks of visual art on almost every count. The absence of figures meant that still life was considered to be non-didactic in content and essentially decorative in character. Although the *Vanitas* still life was a notable exception in this respect, these subjects had waned in the rational age of the eighteenth century and Meléndez is not known to have painted any such works. The inferior status of still life was also dependent on its ordinary, inconsequential subject matter and the belief that it was easy to copy inanimate objects directly from nature in a realistic style.

Meléndez's academic training meant that he was all too aware of the theoretical prejudices against still life. In this respect,

the pseudo-scientific rationale he gave to his still life series for the Prince of Asturias can be regarded as a significant attempt to raise the status of the genre in the eyes of his contemporaries. This was surely helped too by the intended scope and the prestige of this royal commission. However, Meléndez was also extremely proud of his skill as a still life painter per se. The document of 1778 finalising Meléndez's payments for his royal series of still lifes, cited earlier, particularly noted the high regard the artist had of himself and his work. The fact that Meléndez signed one of his still lifes with a dedication to the honour of god is also a remarkable measure of his pride in his own abilities. It is significant too that Meléndez appears to have worked alone, painting fully autograph pictures, and did not employ assistants to produce workshop versions of his still lifes for a wider market, that would have inevitably debased his reputation. Consequently, the narrow academic view of still life as an inconseq--uential, minor genre would have meant little in practice to a painter of his calibre.

The best of Meléndez's paintings demonstrate his representational virtuosity in the imitation of nature, that was, after all, considered to be the *raison d'être* of still life painting. Analysis of Meléndez's still lifes shows the technical mastery he brought to bear in the creation of his highly naturalistic representations.[26] While some of his still lifes might be considered more successful compositions than others, the quality of their naturalism is never compromised in his paintings. Meléndez excelled in painting fruit, that was the archetypal subject matter of still life painting. In his paintings, he captured with extraordinary accuracy the relative size and shape, colours and texture of a wide range of different fruits, as can be seen in the outstanding fruit still lifes in the present exhibition. Few viewers can remain unimpressed by Meléndez's visual description of melons (cats 8, 27), oranges (cats 6, 7), pears (cat. 33), plums (cats 17, 22, 29), and figs (cats 3, 20), to name only some of the fruits represented in these pictures. One of the most remarkable aspects of Meléndez's naturalism is the exactitude with which he captures the colours of different fruits, as can be seen by comparing the different varieties of plums represented in the pictures in this exhibition (cats 5, 17, 22, 29). Single pieces of fruit that are often represented in the very foreground of Meléndez's still lifes seem to invite the viewer to focus exclusively on this particular aspect of his ability. Bread is one of Meléndez's most distinctive signature motifs, as is demonstrated by the different types of loaves and rolls that appear prominently in the paintings in the present exhibition (cats 1, 3, 9, 10, 12, 17, 22, 26, 32, 35). His representation of other comestibles –

different vegetables, meats and fish – is also extraordinarily skilful. The cauliflower in one of the pictures in this exhibition (cat. 13), for example, is an unforgettable *tour de force* of Meléndez's naturalism. Meléndez himself evidently considered consummate representations the partridge and bream in two pictures from the royal series (cats 37, 39), since he reprised these exactly in a number of autograph variants (cats 38, 40).

The paintings in the present exhibition also provide memorable examples of Meléndez's powers of description in a range of manufactured objects, such as ceramic jugs (cats 9, 12, 22, 40), metal pots and pans (cat. 26,), a wine cooler (cat. 33) and glassware (cat. 10). Moreover, the inclusion of a selection of real objects in the recent Meléndez exhibition in the Prado Museum in Madrid allowed a direct comparison with similar ones in Meléndez's still lifes and left visitors in no doubt as to the accuracy and potency of the artist's visual transcription of things from the life (figs 14, 15, cats 24, 26).[27] Meléndez painted to his strengths

Fig. 14: Bowl, 17th century. Modeled clay, coloured, with floral decoration on burnished cream engobe Height: 8cm; ø 15cm. Tonalá (Guadalajara), Mexico. Madrid, Museo de América

Fig. 15: Chocolate Service, 17th–18th Century, Copper. Height: 19cm; ø 21.5cm; handle 56,5cm. Wooden whisk. 32cm; ø 3.9cm. Madrid, Museo Antropológico Nacional

26 Garrido and Cherry (in print).

27 The objects for the Madrid exhibition were selected by Natacha Seseña, who contributed to the catalogue a ground-breaking essay on Meléndez's still lifes and the material culture of his time, "De lo pintado a lo vivo", Madrid, 2004, pp. 119-153. The photographs of objects reproduced here are taken from this essay.

and therefore concentrated on a relatively limited range of man-made objects and types of objects in his still lifes, presented in ever new compositional arrangements. A number of these appear with surprising frequency in the paintings in this exhibition, as in many other still lifes by the artist; cork-bodied wine coolers, barrels of olives, sweetmeat boxes, baskets, tin funnels, a mortar and pestle, terracotta jugs, ceramic vessels from Alcorcón and Talavera, Valencian ware honey pots, wine bottles, a copper chocolate pot and a silver salver. The extremely high levels of verismilitude that Meléndez attained in his representation of such objects was undoubtedly aided by his familiarity with them in reality as recurring stock elements in his paintings. While these would have been fixed in his visual memory from their repetition in so many of his still lifes, the pictorial evidence suggests that they were studied afresh in most paintings. Honey pots

Fig. 16: *Still Life with Partridges, Condiments and Kitchen Utensils,* Oil on canvas, 41,5 x 62cm Madrid, Juan Abelló collection

of Valencian manufacture appear in five pictures here (cats 5, 6, 7, 23, 24); the same Talavera jug with a yellow border appears in two paintings (cats 22, 32); a dark ceramic oil or vinegar bottle is painted in three pictures (cats 12, 15, 38). The same pieces of utilitarian kitchenware reappear in a number of pictures; for example, a long-handled iron frying pan is represented in different positions in two still lifes with fish and fowl (cat. 37, fig. 16). In choosing such objects, at least in part, as vehicles for his representational skills and for their pictorial value in his compositions, Meléndez's still lifes appear to share something with the works of modern still life painters, such as Paul Cézanne, the Cubists or Giorgio Morandi. The latter, for instance, combined and recombined stock objects in endless compositional variations in works that are relatively free from extra-pictorial concerns and that each time stimulated a renewed experience of painting for the artist and, in turn, for the viewer (fig. 13).

It could be argued that monographic exhibitions of the present kind, that allow many of Meléndez's works to be seen together, can induce a certain feeling of monotony in the viewer. In Meléndez's lifetime, of course, his paintings were dispersed among different collections. The exception was his royal series of forty-four still life paintings for the Prince of Asturias, most of which are today on display in the Museo del Prado. While Meléndez was undoubtedly aware of the risks of repetition in this extensive series and naturally attempted to vary the range of his subject matter, even here a significant number of objects and object types are repeated.

One of the aims of this exhibition, that includes almost the same number of paintings, is precisely to illustrate Meléndez's inventive variations on a limited range of still life themes. Therefore, some of the best pictures from Meléndez's royal series and those for other clients have been brought together in this show for the visual rapport between them in terms of theme, composition and format. These include a group of fruit still lifes painted on small, upright canvases, that is such a distinctive format of the artist (cats 1–7). Two of these in particular are close compositional variations on the same theme, with oranges, honey pot and sweetmeat boxes (cats 6, 7). There are a number of Meléndez's most outstanding kitchen still lifes (cats 8–15) and pictures depicting chocolate and sweetmeats exemplify the theme of the dessert still life (cats 24, 25, 26). A group of paintings illustrating Meléndez's landscape format still lifes is presided over by two spectacular works of this type from the royal collection (cats 27–31).

Similarities between Meléndez's still lifes might be explained by their having been painted at the same time; many certainly appear to be closely linked in a chain of creative thought. One of the most striking examples of Meléndez's inventive variations on a theme, however is shown by the relationship between *Still Life with Patridge* for the collection of the Prince of Asturias (cat. 39) and another version of the subject for another client (fig. 16), in which the composition has been radically revised. Reflections in the glass bottles in some of Meléndez's still lifes show the window of the room in which the picture was ostensibly painted (cats 9, 32; fig. 17).

Fig. 17: Luis Meléndez, *Still Life with Apples, Bread, Cheese and Kitchen Utensils*
Oil on canvas, 42 x 62,5 cm
Madrid, Prado Museum, no. 917

This is an important rhetorical detail, that constitutes a "proof" of the artist's presence in a real room and before a real still life arrangement, just as the theoretical construction of still life as a literal copy of nature maintained. However, Meléndez's working practice and occasional use of motifs recycled from his other pictures shows that not all of his paintings were first-hand responses to observed reality. There was, in fact, nothing unusual in this, since it was also the practice of the earliest known still life painters in Spain and elsewhere. The present exhibition breaks new ground in bringing together for the first time a number of Meléndez's variants, in which he repeated versions of his own prototypes (cats 38, 39). In these paintings, the primary motifs were copied from one picture to another, with the addition of other elements. This meant that the variant amounted to a new invention by the artist and therefore still embodied the quality of uniqueness, that appears to have been of considerable importance to Meléndez. While Meléndez imitated nature directly in most of his pictures, in his variants he copied his own motifs, with virtually no loss in naturalism in these. Indeed, judging the paintings in this exhibition on their individual merits, it is extremely difficult, not to say impossible, to detect the recycled motifs in any of them. Whatever the actual source of a motif in Meléndez's still lifes, his paintings amount to the same naturalistic experience for viewers due to the fact that all of the motifs were ultimately studied from nature and therefore carried the conviction of something observed from the life.

The simplified account of still life painting in art theory should not blind viewers to the degree of contrivance in these pictures. In Meléndez's still lifes, the objects may have been observed from the life, but paramount pictorial factors governed their

Fig. 18: Salvador Dalí, *Basket of Bread*, 1926
Oil on canvas, 31,3 x 31,3 cm
St. Petersburg (Florida),
Salvador Dalí Museum

28 Bryson, 1990, chapter 2, on the gaze of the still life painter.

choice, composition and the quality of their naturalistic treatment. The care that Meléndez took to maximise the aesthetic potential of his compositions has already been discussed. The abiding conventions of still life painting itself, such as the representation of objects from a relatively low, close viewpoint, encouraged artists to scrutinise everyday objects in ways that were divorced from the experience of these in reality. The unblinking intensity of Meléndez's contemplative gaze, therefore, delights, surprises and intrigues viewers by revealing qualities of commonplace objects that are recognisably real, but are normally not perceived and taken for granted in lived experience.[28] An obvious manifestation of this is Meléndez's meticulous description of the particularities and detail of each object he represents. Indeed, the inherent strange-ness of this approach was shown by Salvador Dalí in Meléndez-like still lifes of familiar subjects painted with an uncanny hyper-realism (fig. 18).

The traditional character of Meléndez's style in still life painting is highlighted by comparison with the works of his French contemporary Jean-Siméon Chardin (1699-1779) (figs 19, 20, 21). Chardin painted similar still life themes as Meléndez, but frequently painted on relatively small canvases and represented objects as noticeably smaller than the life. In his paintings, objects are mediated by ambient light and atmosphere, that takes account of the realities of optical experience in ways that Meléndez did not. The assertive presence of the paint itself in Chardin's still lifes is another feature of his art that differs significantly from Meléndez's approach.

Fig. 19: Jean-Baptiste-Siméon Chardin,
Still Life with Silver Goblet
Oil on canvas, 33 x 41 cm
Paris, Musée du Louvre

Fig. 21: Jean-Baptiste-Siméon Chardin,
Still Life with Evening Meal and Kitchen Utensils
Oil on copper, 33 x 41 cm
Paris, Musée du Louvre

Fig. 20: Jean-Baptiste-Siméon Chardin,
Still Life with Pear, Nut and Glass of Wine
Oil on canvas, 33 x 41 cm
Paris, Musée du Louvre

Fig. 22: José López Enguídanos,
Still Life with Hare, Watermelon and Lemon
Oil on canvas, 51 x 68 cm
Madrid, Real Academia de Bellas
Artes de San Fernando

The still lifes of Francisco de Goya (1746-1828) are more radically different still in terms of their technique, since the objects appear subsumed within the rich, dynamically handled paint itself, as can be seen by comparing the bream painted by both artists (cats 37, 38; fig. 59). Goya knew Meléndez's series for the Prince of Asturias when these were transferred to the royal palace of Aranjuez the 1790s, but his own still life paintings announce a modern subjectivity in approach that would seem to be at odds with the traditional objectivity of Meléndez's descriptive style of painting. It was, in fact, the latter that survived in Spanish still life painting after his death, as can be seen in the works of the academician José López Enguídanos (1760-1812) (fig. 22).

The illusion of volume and texture in Meléndez's representation of objects in his still lifes powerfully evokes tactile sensations in viewers, especially in pictures whose objects were familiar to contemporaries through handling and use. This is particularly effective in "tonal" paintings in which the objects are cast in a reduced palette of earths, such as *Still Life with Oranges, Walnuts and Boxes of Sweetmeats* (cat. 34) and the sombre, muted chromatic range of *Still Life with Fruit, Bread, Cheese and Wine* (cat. 35). Meléndez demonstrates his descriptive powers by discriminating with his brush between the particular material textures of the carefully chosen and arranged objects in his still lifes, contrasting, for instance, rough with smooth, hard with soft, opaque with shiny. This is particularly successful in compositons where the objects are closely juxtaposed. Some paintings, however, are orchestrated as variations on particular textural themes. In *Still Life with Melon, Jug and Bread* (cat. 8), for instance, Meléndez has painted a range of objects of analagous rough textures, in the reticulated surface of the melon, coarsely textured earthenware and rough nap of the cloth. *Still Life with Herrings, Spring Onions, Bread and Kitchen Utensils* (cat. 12) is a study of light playing on the intricate, rugged surfaces of different comestibles and vessels, painted in a palette of earth tones.

In the earliest dated picture in the exhibition (cat. 1), Meléndez not only contrasts the form, scale and colour of objects, but the range of textures too, in the fruit skins, ceramic vessels, bread crust and glass. In one of Meléndez's best-known compositions, *Still Life with Salmon, Lemon and Kitchen Utensils* (cat. 36), a piece of soft, wet, glistening fish is placed on the hard, dry tabletop and is accompanied by a few objects of metal and clay. The rough surfaces of coarse Alcorcón earthenware provide an effective foil to the textures of other objects in many of Meléndez's still lifes; in pictures in this exhibition, this pottery is placed alongside smooth, richly coloured skins of tomatoes (cat. 14), the soft plumage of birds (cats 39, 40) and objects of different metals (cat. 36). The brown, pitted cork surface of the wine cooler also serves this purpose and in one fruit still life in this exhibition provides a marked contrast with glass, wickerwork and with luminous, richly-coloured pears (cat. 33). *Still Life with Box of Jelly, Bread, Salver, Glass and Winecooler* (cat. 25), painted for the Prince of Asturias, is a *tour de force* of observation of the behaviour of light in transparent glass and its reflections in the pieces of silver and jelly, that is contrasted with the opaque, pitted surfaces of bread and the cork of the wine cooler. The behaviour of light on glassware had intrigued still life painters for centuries; such motifs were emblematic of the painter's engagement with the complex world of visual phenomena and a test of their virtuosity in naturalistic representation.

Ceramic and metal objects are combined in a number of kitchen still lifes (cats 12, 15,) and dessert paintings (cat. 26). Meléndez differentiates between the types of glaze of ceramic objects in his paintings and the smooth, gleaming surfaces of glazed pottery forms a central point of textural contrast for the other objects in a number of works (cats 5-7, 22, 32), as does the fragile, reflective surface of glassware (cats 3, 32, 33, 35). In other pictures, objects of different metals are represented together; tin and beaten

Fig. 23: Cooking pot, 18th century
Fired clay, glazed interior and with an exterior slip
Height: 37.5cm; opening: 19.5; ø 32 cm
Alcorcón (Madrid). Madrid, private collection

Fig. 24: Winecooler,
Cork with wooden bands,
Madrid, Rosendo Naseiro collection

bronze (cat. 13), beaten copper and bronze (cat. 36) and tin, iron and brass (cat. 37). Meléndez has paid particularly close attention to the colour and textural properties of the three metals that make up a bronze ladle and cauldron in a number of paintings (cats 13, 38).

The choice and treatment of the objects in Meléndez's still life paintings betray his fascination with textural incident. He seems to have relished painting the surface intricacies of bread crusts, rough part-glazed surfaces of Alcorcón earthenware (fig. 23), wood and the pitted surfaces of the cork body of wine coolers (fig. 24). This interest is clear from his treatment of the surface of the kitchen table on which the still life objects rest, that is invariably distressed with the

signs of long use in the preparation of meals. Despite the absence of figures in these paintings, the objects imply a human story through the traces of their domestic history. In the same way, the kitchen objects in a genre painting such as Velázquez's *Old Woman Frying Eggs* (Edinburgh, National Gallery of Scotland) would still tell of domestic activity of the figures even if these were not present in the picture. In his still lifes, Meléndez chose to depict much-handled kitchenware that was perhaps from his own kitchen; dents in metal receptacles show the wear and tear of cooking, wooden spoons have been worn smooth with use, the handle of one has split (cat. 12) and another has burned in part (cat. 39),

Fig. 25: Cooking Pot with Two Handles, 18th century
Fired clay, glazed interior and with an exterior slip
Height 24 cm; opening 14.5cm; ø 21.5cm
Alcorcón (Madrid). Madrid, private collection

marks from uneven firing (cats 8, 40) and Meléndez seems to delight in describing with his brush the spontaneous "volcanic" tide marks of this partly glazed earthenware (fig. 25). The thin sheets of wood used in the construction of sweetmeat boxes have split and broken in some cases. Perhaps most significantly of all, the prominent signs of decay that Meléndez paints in different fruits in his pictures show that this is the natural condition of mature fruit, that was commonly seen before the advent of pesticides in modern times (cats 28, 33). In fixing on such key rhetorical details, Meléndez conveys the conviction that he painted things as they really were on a table before him in the kitchen/studio. The aesthetic of Meléndez's still lifes seems to be the antithesis of the classical values of figure painting that were inculcated by the Academy at the time; contrary to generalised, idealised forms, Meléndez insists on the condition of still life as an unadulterated and particularised visual record of objects from the imperfect world of reality.

Meléndez included items of genteel tableware in the dessert still lifes that he occasionally painted and in some of his paintings for the Prince of Asturias (cats 24, 25, 26). However, the utilitarian subject matter that was habitual in his kitchen still lifes would have appeared shockingly banal to most of his contemporaries. Why, then, would the comparatively well-off owners of Meléndez's pictures wish to see painted everyday kitchenware and ordinary foodstuffs? This was, to a great extent, ingrained in the traditional themes of still life painting itself. Fruit still lifes, that represented one of the most attractive faces

the glaze at the edges of earthenware pottery is chipped and kitchen cloths are frayed (cat. 37). A wicker basket in another still life has been thriftily repaired with string (cat. 13). Shards of broken pottery, that are almost "archaeological" reminders of the perpetual life of the kitchen, are used to stop jugs and their eroded edges betray long service in this way (cats 9, 12, 36, 40,).

Meléndez also represents with candour the material imperfections of the objects before him. Attention has been paid to the accidental marks caused in the potting and glazing of earthenware: potting flaws impair the pristine white surfaces of jugs (cats 1, 22) and plates (cat. 29), and the body of terracotta jugs (cat. 34.); Alcorcón jugs show the burn of nature, were the most familiar type of still life paintings and had been from the very origins of the revived genre in modern times. Kitchen still lifes also traditionally represented humble everyday utensils and common foodstuffs. Apart from the decorative value of still life paintings, the inevitable associations of their subject matter with cooking and eating means that they contain a euphoric and sensual message that guarantees them wide appeal. Potent taste sensations are evoked by gazing at Meléndez's luscious fruits and the prime ingredients of meals, as fresh as they day that they were painted, that viewers can mentally "cook". In drawing on memory experiences of meals past and the promise of those to come, the paintings offer life-affirming vicarious pleasure. The perenially reassuring presence of food that such paintings provided for their owners is perhaps most heartfelt in Meléndez's depictions of bread, the traditional "staff of life". Moreover, Meléndez's signature and dedication "to the honour of God" of *Still Life with Partridges, Condiments and Kitchen Utensils* of 1772 (fig. 16) converted it into a form of *exvoto*.[29] This inscription made the picture into an homage to the Creator, to whom the artist owed his gifts, and situated its subject matter of foodstuffs in the context of the Christian belief in God as beneficent Creator of nature as sustenance for mankind.

However, the ultimate value of these works for Meléndez's most discerning contemporaries was aesthetic, as it remains today. Art history from classical antiquity to modern times celebrated artists who had earned fame and fortune for their artistic virtuosity in paintings of humble subjects. The example of Diego Velázquez's *bodegones*

would certainly have been a relevant precedent to eighteenth century Spanish painters, since his *Waterseller* (London, Apsley House) was in the Spanish royal collection. Consequently, in Meléndez's still lifes it is not the intrinsic value or beauty of the actual commonplace objects that viewers are asked to admire, since such trivial things as kitchen utensils and basic foodstuffs in their raw state in themselves had no real aesthetic value. Rather, it is Meléndez's transformation of these objects into an aesthetic experience that is valued; in short, his artistry in the imitation of nature.

After Meléndez's works for the choirbooks of the Royal Chapel ended in 1758, he became a *de facto* specialist in still life painting. The commission from the Prince of Asturias for an extensive series of still lifes on the natural history of Spain was the central event in his later career and his last dated still life painting from this series is exhibited on this occasion (cat. 15). After this project was terminated in 1776, Meléndez evidently continued to paint still lifes for private collectors. He was probably able to interest collectors in his works by capitalising on his reputation as painter to the Prince, as his variants on paintings from the royal series included in the present exhibition suggest. A number of large format fruit still lifes here also show the outstanding calibre of Meléndez's works for clients other than the Prince (cats 32–35); the exceptional scale and quality of one of these in particular suggests that it was painted for an important collector, whose identity remains unknown (cat. 35).

29 Madrid, 2004, cat. 34.

Fig. 26: Pablo Picasso,
Still Life with Jug and Apples, 1919
Oil on canvas, 65 x 43 cm
Paris, Musee Picasso

On his death in 1780, however, Meléndez declared himself a pauper, leaving his wife María Redondo as his executor and heir, who also died a pauper in the following year.[30] Meléndez's declaration of poverty is likely to have been more of a legal recourse than an absolute reality, since such notarial documents served as a straightforward and economical form of will at the time, that were designed to avoid unneccesary legal process and claims on the estate. On the other hand, it may also be reasonable to assume that this did describe to some extent the reduced circumstances of the artist at the natural end of his career.

Meléndez had evidently envisioned his career differently and yearned for the status and opportunities that the position of royal painter would have provided. He was unable to follow in the footsteps of his father as a court painter of miniatures, nor in those of his uncle, Miguel Jacinto Meléndez, who had enjoyed a successful career as a court portraitist, as well as being a major painter of religious pictures. His paintings for the choirbooks of the Royal Chapel were not well known, since these were kept under lock and key in the chapel for use in divine services. His aspirations to work on a large scale remained unproved. Meléndez does not appear to have ever received a commission for a public work of art, such as an altarpiece in a Madrid church, that would have secured him a reputation at court as a figurative artist and not even cabinet sized religious paintings are known by him today. He did not turn to painting genre subjects that were becoming fashionable by the 1770s, although some of his still lifes intersect with themes of outdoor picnics that were common in genre scenes at this time (cats 29–31; fig. 66). However, Meléndez was fully conscious of his strengths in still life and he did become the most original Spanish painter of his time in this genre.

The central irony of Meléndez's career is that his artistic legacy was the product of adverse professional circumstances and had so little to do with his unrealised artistic ambitions. The rediscovery of Meléndez's portrait of the reigning monarch Charles III underneath one of his greatest still life paintings (cat. 34) is an eloquent expression of this. In autobiographical terms, there is a world of difference between Meléndez's *Self*

30 Tufts, 1985, pp. 32, 216-8.

Portrait (fig. 1) and his subsequent still life paintings, where the youthful aspirations for public acclaim within the art establishment contrast with the introverted domesticity of the kitchen and the privacy of the studio. Meléndez, however, has come into his own in modern times, in the wake of developments in *avant-garde* painting where the still life became an expressive vehicle for some of the most creative artists (fig. 26). These works have forcibly shown audiences today the irrelevance of the academic hierarchy of genres that prevailed in Meléndez's own time and consequently have allowed a fuller appreciation of his talents in this field. While Meléndez at the end of his life may have looked back ruefully over his frustrated career and the twists of fate that forced him to specialise in still life painting, his proud nature would have been gratified by the thought that exhibitions such as the present one were to set out to celebrate his extraordinary achievement.

Meléndez and the development of Spanish and European still life painting in the Eighteenth Century
Juan J. Luna

Until recently, the eighteenth century was considered to be the 'least Spanish' of the major eras in the history of Spanish art in general, and the history of painting in particular, despite the significant constellation of masters working at the time. This assumption prevailed across the entire cultural spectrum of the century and, although there was some truth to it, it was no more than received opinion born of ignorance and superficial appearance rather than reality. Modern research has brought about a dramatic change of perspective, uncovering new artists and reassessing the contribution of well-known names of the period through an approach which is more methodological than before and, as a consequence, more balanced.[1] Analyses of the socio-economic circumstances of the years 1700-1808, the political problems existing between states – the strategic conflicts and dynastic rivalries – tend to distinguish between foreign influences and the intrinsically Spanish context, which was evolving in a positive direction.[2] As a result, this indisciplinary approach has brought to critical appreciation the pictorial richness of the eighteenth century in Spain and challenged the traditional interpretation of the period.[3]

A New Dynasty: The House of Bourbon

On 16 November 1700, in the sumptuous surroundings of the Palace of Versailles, the Duke of Anjou was recognised as King of Spain during a solemn ceremony presided over by his grandfather, Louis XIV of France. This event marked the beginning of a new era in Western Europe. One particular remark made, on the occasion, by the Marquis of Castelldosríus, the Spanish ambassador, to the effect that 'Now there are no Pyrenees' became a cliché expressing a future desire for collaboration at all levels. This was in stark contrast to the attitude which had prevailed for decades before. Up until that moment, relations between the two kingdoms had been characterised by confrontation and an apparent lack of cultural exchange. Thus, the young monarch, Philip V, faced numerous difficulties on taking possession of his Spanish inheritance. Even so, the diplomat's famous phrase was not just timely, but indeed prophetic, at least for the next century or so. The trans--formations which began with the Bourbon accession to the Spanish throne were profound and far-reaching, and they led to the introduction of a wide range of new ideas from continental Europe.[4] This, in turn, produced tremendous tensions (especially intense in a country where religion was intimately linked to both society and the world of art), so that the Spanish Enlightenment was inflected with numerous inconsistencies and has its own particular character.

In the Iberian Peninsula, as in other parts of Europe, a gulf opened up between official

1 Kulber and Soria, 1959; Sánchez Cantón, 1965; Camón Aznar, Morales and Valdivieso, 1984.

2 Desdevizes du Dezert, 1897-1904; Anes, 1969; Anes, 1975; Omínguez Ortiz, 1976; Plaza Prieto, 1976; Bottineau, 1993a.

3 Bottineau, 1993a; Herr, 1971; Sarrailh, 1974; Pérez Sánchez, 1988; Morales y Marín, 1994.

4 Scéaus, 1993; Saule, 1996; Mahón-Madrid, 2002-2003.

art and popular art and, at the same time, there was evident resistance to foreign influence in important sectors of the Church and nobility. It was the bourgeoisie, newly emergent at that time, which attempted to direct the new and regenerative ideas, but its initial weakness, aggravated by the political crisis at the close of the eighteenth century, prevented it from playing a truly dominant role.

An Overview of the Arts

In the fascinating artistic panorama of the eighteenth century, certain key convergences stand out. The House of Bourbon did nothing to inhibit or transform the immediate atmosphere in which religious architecture evolved. The latter, full of national motifs, was Baroque in its decorative schemes but rarely so in its functional design. It was conceived and realised by masters who had begun their artistic work in the seventeenth century and whose formation reflected the key principles of the second half of that century. These artists arrived at the peak of their creative and technical careers in the eighteenth century.[5] Their style, popularly known as *churrigueresque* (an advanced, highly ornamental form of the Baroque), is exemplary of the state of tension between the Baroque and a generalised European classicism coming from Italian and French artists.[6] Similarly, in sculpture, wood painting and the important activities of workshops producing religious images the splendid aesthetic impulse of the Golden Age continued.[7] The initial rupture with tradition, which would be the most centralised of the changes of the period, occurred in painting.[8]

The cosmopolitan nature of art in the eighteenth century Madrid court continues to surprise historians and researchers of the period alike. The important foreign influences – of Italian, French, and other European origin – partially eclipsed the various traditional arts which stagnated, despite retaining a certain official support. As a result, some historians fail to appreciate the problematic nature of the forces in conflict during this period and assume that they powerfully affected eighteenth century Spanish culture, thus internationalizing it but depriving it of part of its inherently Hispanic foundations.[9] Many artists imitated whatever innovation arrived from over the Pyrenees, and hence appeared relatively strange because of their desire to adopt new fashions and ignore established Spanish tradition.[10] The splendid triumphs of the Golden Age – the achievements of great and formidable personalities and characterised by a strong sense of originality – had prevailed in seventeenth century art and literature despite the period's enormously complex social, economic, political, military and dynastic difficulties. In contrast, eighteenth century Spain, with its new monarch of French origin, appeared to the critics to be excessively foreign and lacking in native peninsular roots.[11] It seemed, moreover, that foreigners monopolised key positions in the art world from the time of the accession of Philip V to the throne until the reign of Charles III; it was only towards the end of the century – rather like a rare and exotic flower blooming in a desert – that the titanic figure of Goya appeared, marking a complete rupture with the earlier period.

5 Kubler, 1957; Chueca Goitia, 1971; Tovar Martín, 1979.

6 Rodríguez Gutiérrez de Ceballos, 1971.

7 Gómez Moreno, 1951; Gómez Moreno, 1958; Sánchez Cantón, 1965; Otero Túñez, 1980; Martín González, 1983.

8 Aguilera, 1946; Lafuente Ferrari, 1947; Lafuente Ferrari, 1953; Sullivan, 1982.

9 Gaya Nuño, 1970.

10 Orozco Díaz, 1947; Bordeaux-Paris-Madrid, 1979-1980; Pérez Sánchez, 1988; Morales y Marín, 1994.

11 Bottineau, 1993a.

Nevertheless, such interpretations can no longer be sustained. Detailed studies[12] of the period in its entirety have revealed a multi-faceted picture, more profound, more complete, and more objective, than previously thought, This allows a better understanding of the era without the need to reject the prevailing, undeniably cosmopolitan, ambience.[13] As a result, researchers have begun to re-evaluate the role of previously unacknowledged Hispanic influences, which never totally disappeared. There was a resurgence in these traditional Spanish styles during the reign of Philip V, they achieved a significant role under Ferdinand VI, and later flourished under Charles III and Charles IV. Over time, Spanish authors became less and less traditional, drawing inspiration from foreign colleagues,[14] from whom they borrowed new ideas to modernise their own art without losing their characteristic originality, which was frequently conservative. They thus developed a singular and distinctive style that was charming and graceful, unlike the key international movements of the time.[15]

As in other European countries, this artistic renaissance was centred on the court, whilst the provinces remained anchored to outmoded aesthetic principles. But the art of the court was linked to a particular dynasty, to the key personages of the time, and to their vicissitudes: it was thus prey to matrimonial alliances, family relationships, and political, cultural and advisory connections with their attendant struggles for power and influence at all levels. As a consequence, it was conditioned by luck and opportunity, and, in many cases, was the result of a series of coincidences. From another perspective,

the historical climate did play a dominant role, imperceptibly influencing many of the essential tendencies of the era. Thus, the art of the court was nourished in two ways: first, by whimsical unpredictability; second, by its relationship with the political structures of the epoch and their special circumstances. With regard to the latter, it was essentially a question of whether or not these had been imposed from without.

The Spanish eighteenth century, therefore, depended greatly upon the different principles, attitudes and conditions which shaped its history: the accession of Philip V and his lengthy reign (1700-1746); the peaceful and constructive era of Ferdinand VI (1746-1759), sadly all too short; the innumerable transformations which occurred under Charles III (1759-1788); and, lastly, the situation, at first excellent but later more critical, under Charles IV. His reign began favourably in 1788, but deteriorated over the course of the final decade of the century, and ended with the dramatic dethroning of the monarch, the tragic cataclysm of the French invasion, and the beginning of the devastating War of Independence in 1808.

Numerous economic factors determined conditions in eighteenth century Spain. In a period of European prosperity, which contrasted with the depression of the seventeenth century, both the Spanish monarchy and the kingdom as a whole enjoyed a period of expansion and progress which greatly improved the economic situation. This explains why monarchs of the House of Bourbon enjoyed a privileged financial situation denied to Philip III, Philip IV or Charles III. It permitted them

12 Luna, 1979; Bottineau, 1986.

13 Urrea Fernández, 1977.

14 Préclin, 1952; Junquera y Mato, 1979; Morales y Morín, 1994.

15 Mousnier, Labrousse and Bouloiseau, 1953; Mahón-Madrid, 2002-2003.

to construct magnificent royal residences (the Royal Palace in Madrid and the Palace of La Granja de San Ildefonso, amongst others) and to improve or extend existing ones (those of Aranjuez, El Prado, and El Escorial), as well as building wonderful masterpieces of refinement and good taste, such as the little palaces or *casitas* adjacent to some of the aforementioned monuments.[16] It also allowed them to contract foreign artists – some mediocre, others illustrious – who shone in contrast to homegrown architects, sculptors, painters, decorators and highly qualified craftsmen. They put together enormous collections of pictures,[17] sculptures, and artifacts commissioned in Spain or beyond. They founded centres for the manufacture of decorative arts which were maintained with exhaustive funds: the Santa Bárbara Royal Tapestry Workshop, where Spanish artists in general, and painters in particular, learned their trade;[18] the La Granja Royal Glass and Crystal Workshop,[19] which supplied the palaces with splendid pieces; and the Buen Retiro Royal Porcelain Workshop.[20] To these impressive royal institutions can be added the Alcora ceramic workshop, belonging to the Counts of Aranda.[21]

Following the example of the monarchs, aristocrats and merchants renewed their patronage of the arts and ordered a variety of commissions consonant with their interests and personal possibilities. The Church, with an increase in its income, and bolstered by a favourable financial situation, thanks to a rise in donations to its already extensive patrimony, also initiated a period of activities in keeping with the rhythm of the century. It thus built, extended and redecorated many institutions.

Despite all of this, the idea of general prosperity must be qualified by the fact that, in the first third of the century, wars and economic reforms mutually neutralised their respective negative and positive effects. It was in the decade 1730-1740 that the economy improved to a notable degree, reaching a peak during the rule of Ferdinand VI, and even later. In the final years of the reign of Charles III, his pursuit of a major international role for Spain began to adversely affect the royal coffers. This critical situation worsened under Charles IV, initially as a consequence of the confrontation with revolutionary France, and afterwards with England, which resulted in the instability of commercial trade with the American colonies, and finally with the spread of epidemics and a series of poor harvests between 1794 and 1805.

The Atmosphere in the Visual Arts

Returning to the art world, and specifically to the world of painting, it is appropriate to describe here some of the circumstances of the transition from the seventeenth to eighteenth centuries in Spain.[22] With the death of Charles II, the last of the Spanish Hapsburgs, in 1700, the last trace of the splendid series of artists who worked in Madrid, Seville, Granada, Valencia, and other regional centres during the Golden Age seemed to disappear too. Very few were born in that era who worked for the House of Bourbon. A brief survey reveals that in the last two decades of the seventeenth century numerous painters of reputation died: Juan Rizi (1681), Bartolomé Esteban Murillo (1682), Antonio Arias (1684), Francisco Rizi (1685), Francisco de Herrera the Younger

16 Kulber, 1957.

17 Madrazo, 1884; Luna, 1993.

18 Benedito y Vives, 1926; Held, 1971; Bartolomé, 1999.

19 Ruiz Alcón, 1969; Bartolomé, 1999.

20 Martínez Caviró, 1973; Mañueco Santurtún, 1999; Bartolomé, 1999.

21 Ainaud de Lasarte, 1952; Casanovas, 1989; Summa Artis XLV, 1999; Mañueco Santurtún, 2003.

22 Bottineau, 1993a.

(1685), Juan Carreño de Miranda (1685), Ignacio Iriarte (1685), Antonio van de Pere (1688), José Jiménez Donoso (1690), Sebastián Muñoz (1690), Juan de Valdés Leal (1690), Pedro Atanasio Bocanegra (1689), Claudio Coello (1693), Juan de Sevilla (1695), Pedro Núñez de Villavicencio (1700), and others whose names need not appear here.[23] Those who survived into the eighteenth century are few, and they only did so for a brief period, with none of them bringing anything of importance to the art world. Amongst these figured Antonio Palomino (1655-1726) who, along with some contemporary painters from Seville, Granada and Madrid, formed part of a group better known for its contribution to the theory of art than for its paintings. In any case, as time passes current research adds ever more information with which to evaluate this period. Although there are no documentary sources to suggest the existence of previously unknown distinguished artists, there are signs of a number who inherited their sense of creativity from the formal principles of that earlier century in which they were born and to which they owed their artistic principles, even though they always remained inferior to what was occurring on the other side of the Pyrenees.

Evidently, the arrival of a new dynasty brought with it important changes which were neither sudden nor all of equal significance. The Baroque style of the seventeenth century continued to flourish at the Madrid court,[24] but the slow appearance of French and Italian artists helped to modernise it. The presence of Luca Giordano in Madrid until 1702, together with the work of Palomino, ensured a continuation of Baroque decorative styles; nevertheless, the most popular cultivators of these were well-intentioned painters of lesser talent. Amongst them was Miguel Jacinto Meléndez,[25] the uncle of Luis Egidio Meléndez. One must recognise that his religious compositions display a certain elegance; and his portraits, often routine and rather superficial, possess a certain value for their iconography, although they are not of the same standard as those by his European contemporaries. However, other painters gradually emerged whose modest works became the point of departure for later developments. The journeys which some of them made to Italy,[26] along with a new vigour resulting from the frequent introduction of pictures from outside the country, and the works of artists of French and Italian origin, had a positive effect. It was decided to create an Academy of Fine Arts, following the French model,[27] and a preparatory commission was set up in advance of its foundation, in 1752, during the reign of Ferdinand VI. Thus was born the San Fernando Royal Academy of Fine Arts in Madrid, whose example was followed during the second half of the eighteenth century in various places in Spain. This institution would be the corner stone of the official transformation of Hispanic art.[28]

Still Life Painting

In order to determine the importance and interest of Spanish still life painting in the eighteenth century,[29] it must be pointed out that it was precisely around 1700 that the term *bodegón* was first defined in Spain.[30] In the first volume of his *Museo pictórico*, dated 1715,[31] Palomino discussed the development of painting throughout

23 Angulo Íñigo, 1971; Camón Aznar, 1977; Pérez Sánchez, 1988.

24 Bottineau, 1993a; Urrea Fernández, 1973.

25 Santiago Páez, 1966; Santiago Páez, 1989; Ovideo-Madrid, 1989-1990.

26 Waterhouse, 1969 and 1976; Wittkower, 1973.

27 Montaiglon, 1875; Fontaine, 1914.

28 Sánchez Cantón, 1952; Bédat, 1974.

29 Lafuente Ferrari, 1935; Cherry, 1999.

30 Calvo Serraller, 1981.

31 Palomino and Velasco, 1947.

history using the following terminology: '*bodegón*: a type of painting which represents all that is edible'; '*bodegoncillo*: a little *bodegón*', and '*florero*: a flower painting'.[A] Although this type of painting appeared in Spain towards the end of the sixteenth century,[32] artists and writers of artistic treatises mention these themes[33] with a different nomenclature,[34] adopting at times different terms for the subjects represented: *vanitas*, hieroglyphics, fruits or fruit bowls, flower vases, larders, *bodegoncillos*, garlands, festoons, etc.[35] Golden Age literature makes multiple references to these variations as representations of nature, as excellent imitations of the visible world and, some--times, as significant carriers of symbolic moral messages,[36] these being particularly evident in cases of *trompe l'oeil* techniques.[37] Lope de Vega, Carducho, and Pacheco mentioned compositions of this type, and in more than one inventory of Golden Age

paintings similar allusions may be found,[38] revealing its popularity.[39] The term *bodegón* becomes generalised in the eighteenth century, and the variant *naturaleza muerta* seems to derive from the French term, *nature morte*, in the nineteenth century,[40] being a literal calque on both French and English.[41]

The situation of still life painting at the beginning of the eighteenth century was analogous to that of religious painting, decorative works, and portraits. No notable transformations occurred in general taste, nor did appreciable signs of development appear in these different forms. No artist stood out for his importance or creativity, although, as in other areas of painting, individuals with a certain aesthetic ability did continue to follow the basic precepts as they had been laid down in the splendour of the Golden Age,[42] and this culminated in the influence of the Neapolitan Baroque.[43] Curiously, the death of the Neapolitan,

32 Cassou, 1952; Bayón, 1970.

33 Bye, 1921.

34 Faré, 1975.

35 Cavestany, 1936-1940.

36 Gállego, 1972.

37 Vega, 1980.

38 Sánchez Cantón, 1931-1943.

39 Brown, 1978.

40 Newark, 1964-1965.

41 Bergström, 1970.

42 Torres Martín, 1971; Pérez Sánchez, 1983-1984.

43 Pérez Sánchez, 1965; Sestieri, 2000; Gregori, 2003.

Fig. 27: Giuseppe Recco,
Still Life with Fish and Turtle, c.1680
Oil on canvas, 75 x 103 cm
Madrid, Prado Museum, no. 319

Fig. 28: Andrea Belvedere,
Vase of Flowers and a Bird
Oil on canvas, 77 x 65 cm
Madrid, Prado Museum, no. 569

Giuseppe Recco (fig. 27), in Alicante in 1695 did not just fail to interrupt this trend, but in fact gave it new force, since his daughter Elena and son Nicola Maria continued in the tradition of their father. The works of Andrea Belvedere (c.1652-1732) (fig. 28) possessed a similar importance; his canvases, destined both for the Royal Collection and private individuals, displayed clear pre-eighteenth century characteristics:[44] light backgrounds, a wide colour palette, an easy decorative style, and a monumentality in composition with a certain pre-Rococo jovial lightness of spirit. Amongst the most esteemed works of that time are those by Margarita Caffi (1650/51-1710), full of joy, grace, and contrasts, as well as pictures by lesser-known painters who worked with the same pleasant, almost dreamy expressive mode. These productions marked the beginning of a new age, one more open to refinement, in contrast with the colossal, theatrical grandiosity of the previous century.[45]

On the other hand, in contrast to what occurred with Italian – and particularly Neapolitan – influences, one cannot speak of a French presence in works of this nature in Spanish collections. From this there derives an almost total poverty in relation to the great richness of still life painting in that school which produced so many valuable and exquisite works. These were sometimes pompous and spectacular, at other times intimate and direct, and executed by excellent artists who worked for the court and the urban bourgeoisie in Paris and other large French cities.

Still Life Painting in Madrid at the Beginning of the Eighteenth Century

In Madrid, no name of true importance stands out amongst those who devoted themselves to the specialism of still life. The Royal Collections and the collections of the nobility abound in still lifes, mainly of Dutch and Italian origin, as well as from the Spanish Golden Age. Although they constituted a permanent source of inspiration for artists, they also represented a powerful bastion of traditions difficult to overcome for those painters seeking innovation. Another source were the ever-present compositions of Luca Giordano (1634-1705),[46] rich in their combinations of objects placed in secondary positions (sometimes in the foreground) and which were doubtless studied by Antonio Palomino, as can be appreciated in the different motifs of this kind which appear in his works.

Palomino merits special attention. In the *Museo pictórico*[47] mentioned earlier, this painter and author of various treatises dedicated a lengthy chapter to flower and fruit paintings. According to the principles outlined there, he included various of these motifs in his large frescoes and oils; large vases overflowing with a huge variety of flowers, complicated garlands, great bunches of flowers and chains of whimsical forms, all ever more Baroque. The still lifes mentioned in the inventory of Teodoro Ardemans (1665-1726), a painter and architect who had been a disciple of Pereda and Carreño de Miranda, also seemed to have an unquestionably Baroque spirit in keeping with Madrid fashion of the time.[48] In the same vein are the still life studies by Jerónimo Antonio de Ezquerra (dated between 1715 and 1725),

44 Apollonio, 1960; Spike, 1983.

45 Pérez Sánchez, 1967; Causa, 1972.

46 Ferrari and Scavizzi, 1992; Mahón-Madrid, 2002-2003.

47 Gaya Nuño, 1957; Aparicio Olmos, 1966; Pérez Sánchez, 1972.

48 Agulló y Cobo, 1978.

all but unknown to us today. Ceán Bermúdez declares that he 'excelled in *bodegones*',[49] but from the few works, centred on allegorical and religious themes,[50] that have survived, one would conclude that his style was not that different from that of Carreño de Miranda and Palomino, and was probably similar to the works of Pereda and Cerezo. In one of his better known canvases he skilfully combined diverse plants, trees and shrubs with motifs from an aquatic world – fish, tortoises, shells – which recalled similar images in Recco's canvases.[51]

Other painters of lesser quality, like Francisco Pérez Sierra (died 1709), Jerónimo Secano (died 1710) and Lorenzo Montero (died 1710) were also interested in this type of painting and are cited in treatises by authors of the period. As the eighteenth century progressed, artists who specialised in religious painting or in scenes of daily life, like Juan García de Miranda (died 1749)[52] and Valero Iriarte (died c.1744),[53] found themselves obliged to include in their compositions some motifs from still life.[54] However, none of them reflected the new tendencies which, beyond the frontiers of the kingdom, were spreading throughout Europe in line with the principles of French and Italian schools.

Still Life Painting in Andalusia
In Seville the transition from the seventeenth to the eighteenth century was accompanied by a growing interest in the use of *trompe l'oeil* techniques, which were closely connected to Flemish and Dutch examples but also had an Italian origin.[55] Masters like Murillo[56] and Valdés Leal[57] had many followers; the majority, given the importance of Murillo, restricted themselves to slavishly imitating him instead of creating something new.[58] The still life genre was barely affected, except in the details, visible in various canvases of the Sevillian school, which depicted objects of everyday use in the style of Murillo, as can be seen in the works of Juan de Espinal, Domingo Martínez, Juan Ruiz Soriano and others.[59]

Some of these painters executed works which may be considered as still life studies, although there is not the slightest suggestion of substantial innovations.[60] Lucas Valdés (died 1724), the son of Valdés Leal, painted murals with flowers and fruit; Andrés Pérez (died 1727) and Domingo Martínez (died 1750), mentioned above, and Antonio Torres, apparently stood out from their contemporaries for the use of certain details and individual touches, but they did not surpass the general level of mediocrity characteristic of the genre.

One of the most significant artists of the time in Seville was Bernardo Lorente Germán (1680-1759). His formative years were spent under the tutelage of his father and were heavily influenced by Murillo,[61] whose style he imitated, although he also executed works of a certain originality such as the theme of the Divine Shepherdess, a devotional image of the time with profound Franciscan roots. In his works he combined motifs of both Mannerist and Baroque origin, frequently taken from Italy and familiar to him from reproductions. He was also a court portrait painter during the period of its move to Andalusia between 1729 and 1733. As far as his still lifes are concerned, he is known for a use of *trompe l'oeil* in which both symbolic and everyday details play a part; he depicts

49 Ceán Bermúdez, 1965.

50 Luna, 1984.

51 Cavestany, 1936-1940.

52 Trujillo, 1981.

53 Pérez Sánchez, 1982.

54 Battersby, 1974.

55 Junquera y Mato, 1976; Valdivieso, 1986.

56 Angulo Íñiguez, 1980.

57 Kinkead, 1978; Madrid, 1991.

58 Angulo Íñiguez, 1975; Valdivieso, 1986.

59 Valdivieso and Serrera, 1982.

60 Luna 1984.

61 Angulo Íñiguez, 1975.

"corners of the studio" paintings (the nooks and crannies of studios, bottles, ropes, engravings, papers, wax busts, tins, pictures hanging on the wall and objects on shelves). One can see how religious themes gradually become secularised, as occurred with the *vanitas* and similar topics, which were fashionable in the seventeenth century but disappeared in the eighteenth.[62]

Another important painter of this time was Pedro de Acosta,[63] whose works span the years 1741-1755. Judging by his style and the provenance of his pictures, one assumes that he was Sevillian, or at least he can be related to the Sevillian style. He is known for his charming "corners of the studio" type paintings, which combine engravings with a great variety of motifs: musical instruments, kitchen implements, even dead animals such as birds or fish. These pictures reflect his intention of achieving a new refinement; to this end, he emphasises the quality of surfaces as well as the bulk of the objects and the shadows which they project onto the surface on which they are placed. Such works, although not strongly theatrical, betray a reasonably skilled, if rather naïve, hand. The great quantity of resources and the importance of each detail evoke the atmosphere of a Sevillian painter's studio at the beginning of the eighteenth century. Such examples of *trompe l'oeil* reveal the great popularity in Spain of Flemish, Dutch, and French engravings. These same engravings also appear in works by the painter Carlos López – about whose life we know nothing, but whose works are comparable to those of Acosta – and in works by Francisco Gallardo, who is an equally enigmatic figure.

Francisco Gallardo continued to use the pictorial idiom of colleagues from the beginning of the eighteenth century, although he was now working in the second half of it. We know of four canvases from his hand, signed possibly in Cadiz in 1764,[64] which carry to the limit the visual effects developed by Lorente Germán and Acosta. They display his personal interest in literature, with particular inspiration from Cervantes and from poetry. In his paintings one can also see evidence of Flemish, Dutch, and French influences, most especially engravings by Schut, Perelle, and Santerre, as well as themes of the genre such as floral detail and studies of the nude. The traditional idea which lies behind these compositions reflects the success and worth of this particular artist, and also the lack of any new orientation capable of influencing the sensibility of artists and clients in other directions.[65]

Andrés Rubira's still lifes were perhaps different, though they did tend to venerate the successes of the past through an archaizing tendency evocative of a distant tenebrism suited to the depiction of a coarse, primary reality whose key champion in the previous century had been Pedro de Medina Valbuena. He was a disciple of Domingo Martínez and he collaborated with Francisco Vieira in Lisbon, dying in 1760.[66] Unfortunately, his works were lost in the tragic earthquake of 1755 which shook the Portuguese capital.[67] In the opinion of Ceán, 'he excelled in the execution of *bodegones* and *bambochas* [genre paintings], rendered with good taste, humour, and elegance', and his popular compositions were comparable with 'the early Velázquez'.

62 Luna, 1984.

63 Cavestany, 1936-1940; Angulo Íñiguez, 1975; Pérez Sánchez, 1983-1984.

64 Pemán, 1930.

65 Cavestany, 1936-1940; Pérez Sánchez, 1983-1984.

66 Luna, 1973.

67 Ayres de Carvalho, 1960-1962.

Fig. 29: Antonio Viladomat,
Still Life with Game
Oil on canvas, 65 x 100 cm
Barcelona, Museu Nacional d'Art de Catalunya

Fig. 30: Antonio Viladomat,
Still Life with Vegetables and Fish
Oil on canvas, 65 x 100 cm
Barcelona, Museu Nacional d'Art de Catalunya

Still Life Painting in Catalonia and Aragon

The still lifes which we have by the painter Antonio Viladomat (1678-1755) (figs 29, 30) bear witness to the continuation of aesthetic principles from the Golden Age in the territories of the Kingdom of Aragon.[68] Born in Barcelona, this artist was the most important painter in Catalonia[69] during the first half of the eighteenth century.[70] His paintings reveal a realist approach to the depiction of objects, indicating his proximity to the Neapolitan school of the previous century.[71] His intense use of tenebrist lighting, and his tendency to highlight the details of objects with a certain theatricality, anticipated Meléndez's own ideas, more because of their common Neapolitan inspiration than through personal contact, which was probably nonexistent. His creations are highly singular, revealing violent contrasts and a clumsy naturalism, painted freely and with a sombre, rather dry palette. Of great importance in mural paintings of flowers and fruit[72] is also Tomás Ferrer, from Zaragoza, from whom we have works dated to between 1730 and 1760.

Still Life Painting in Valencia and Majorca

Still life painting was not, at first, particularly developed in Valencia, whether due to the lack of interest of patrons or because there were no real artists of significance there. It was, however, the birth place of Vicente Victoria (1650-1713), a disciple of Carlo Maratti, who continued the seventeenth century tradition of Rome and Bologna, and to whom the city paid due homage. The latter combined the painting of frescoes and canvases with his study of letters.[73] As a canon of Játiva cathedral, he painted in the Valencia region, returning later to Rome, where he died. He executed excellent *trompe l'oeil* effects with arms, standards, and various weapons of war and hunting, reaching such a level of skill in his optical illusions that his great understanding of drawing, colour, and lighting is immediately evident.[74] José Fortea and Francisco Grifol are mentioned in eighteenth century treatises as practitioners of this type of painting[75] in murals and canvases respectively, and they also enjoyed a certain prestige in Valencia.[76]

68 Cavestany, 1936-1940.

69 Benet, 1947.

70 Carrera y Pujal, 1951.

71 Alcolea, 1959-1962.

72 Gudiol, Alcolea, and Cirlot, s/d.

73 Blunt, 1967.

74 Pérez Sánchez, 1983-1984.

75 Pérez Sánchez, 1983-1984.

76 Orellana, 1967.

Aside from those painters mentioned above, only one other, Joaquín Eximeno (died c.1754) is worthy of mention. The church of the Pilar in Valencia still retains some of his canvases with spectacular floral arrangements, but they are hastily and clumsily painted and reveal little variation. His archaic style recalls works by Tomás Hiepes, who worked in the mid seventeenth century.

Nevertheless, in the second half of the eighteenth century a powerful school, surprisingly prolific in the execution of floral themes, appeared in Valencia, although the city was not a traditional centre of this type of work, despite examples by a few masters of the seventeenth century. It was due to the growing silk industry, which, as in the case of the French city of Lyons, required numerous designs with garlands, intertwined flowers, and bunches to decorate its yarns.[77]

The Majorcan Guillermo Mesquida (1675-1747) also produced still lifes. He worked outside Spain, having trained in Rome under Maratti, with whom he shared a taste for the opulence of the decorative Baroque. The lack of a definitive study of his work prevents any more than a brief mention of his name in this context.[78] We ought to include here the names of artists such as José Dardarón or Jorge Carbonell (died 1759), since they are cited by the chroniclers of Palma de Majorca as excellent decorators and designers of fruit and flower images, the first for his murals and the second for his fabric designs.[79]

Art During the Reign of Ferdinand VI

Many historians insist that 1746 was a decisive date in the history of Spanish painting, not because this was the year of the death of Philip V but because it marked the birth of Goya.[80] It was also the year of the birth of Luis Paret y Alcázer[81] and Ramón Bayeu,[82] as well as other distinguished artists. Some years earlier Francisco Bayeu (1734),[83] José del Castillo (1737),[84] and Mariano Salvador Maella (1739)[85] had been born. The important generation of the second half of the eighteenth century was already being trained and beginning to develop.[86] Amongst those were Antonio González Ruiz (1711-1785),[87] Antonio González Velázquez (1723-1794),[88] and, above all, the exceptional painter of still lifes, Luis Egidio Meléndez, who, in that very year of 1746, signed his prestigious *Self Portrait*, now in the Louvre in Paris.[89]

From a broader historical perspective, this year marked the beginning of the reign of Ferdinand VI,[90] which was so beneficial in economic and political terms. Spain was slowly recovering, living standards were improving, war wounds were healing, and plans for peace and neutrality succeeded those of war and territorial expansion of the earlier era. New winds blew through the court,[91] and the predominance of French painters (Louis-Michel van Loo would return to Paris and only Charles-Joseph Flipart[92] would remain) gave way to Italians such as Amigoni, Joli, Battaglioli and Giaquinto[93] who, in a sense, took the place of Houasse,[94] Ranc,[95] and Van Loo.[96] Decoration of the Royal Palace in Madrid continued.[97] It was built on the former site of the Hapsburgs' venerable Alcázar, which had been razed by a fire in 1734. Italian opera was in the ascendant,[98] and art collections in royal palaces increased with the incorporation of contemporary works more in keeping with

77 Lyon, 1982.

78 Alomar, 1975.

79 Cavestany, 1936-1940.

80 Gassier and Wilson, 1974; Guidol, 1970; Madrid, 1995-1996.

81 Gaya Nuño, 1952; Delgado, 1957; Salas, 1977; Bilbao, 1991-1992.

82 Morales and Marín, 1979.

83 Morales and Marín, 1979.

84 Sambricio, 1958.

85 Alcolea, 1967.

86 Henares Cuéllar, 1977.

87 Arrese, 1973.

88 Rius Oliva, 1964.

89 Tufts, 1971 and 1982; Luna, 1982 and 1984; Luna 1995.

90 Danvila, 1905.

91 Barrenechea, 1956.

92 Lunam, 1981.

93 Sánchez Cantón, 1916; Urrea Fernández, 1977.

94 Luna, 1981-1982.

95 Luna, 1980.

96 Luna, 1978; Luna, 1982; Luna, 1987.

97 Plaza, 1975.

98 Morales Borrero, 1972.

the Rococo style of the mid century.[99] The influence of the court, whose aesthetic preferences were so different from the Spanish Golden Age tradition,[100] took some time to arrive in the various regions of the kingdom and to infiltrate the different levels of society. The aesthetic taste of the Court made its presence felt through the academies,[101] institutions of great value that served to establish trends, determine influences, fix norms, and educate artistic taste.[102] Significant support derived from the academies' systemization of artistic ideas, which brought with it a certain uniformity. Above all, these institutions raised the social status of the artist, conferring on him the dignity of an academician and offering him a better financial situation and a distinguished role in society, one of the main objectives of the profession from the time of El Greco until well into the eighteenth century.[103]

Concerning Madrid and its court, the San Fernando Academy of Fine Arts, inaugurated in 1752 after laborious negotiations following on from the establishment of its preparatory committee in 1744, was of fundamental importance for the art world. It initiated various cultural activities, which were bolstered by the foundation of other academies in the provinces.[104] This contributed to a consistency in the application of criteria, the spread of a method of instruction based on academic drawing, and the systematic integration of complementary disciplines essential for the proper formation of young artists, all of which made success possible in a time of an appreciably high level of quality and precision.[105] Although the painting of *bodegones* and flowers was not considered comparable to the so-called 'grand themes',

it was not excluded as unsuitable for academic study. Despite being regarded as secondary or inferior, subordinate to other classes of painters, the academies accepted the best practitioners of this genre. They thus enjoyed, at the very least, a physical presence, and their merits were recognised alongside those artists of historical themes who had previously eclipsed them, being more highly valued in line with French fashion.[106]

The Collecting of the Still Lifes at the Madrid Court

Madrid was the best place for studios specializing in still life in the second half of the eighteenth century, thanks to the Academy, to the nucleus of great painters who surrounded the court, and to the, now distant, protection of the second wife of Philip V, Elizabeth Farnese,[107] who had acquired an important private collection which contained various Neapolitan paintings that were very dear to her.[108] As a result of her initial efforts, the Royal Collections contained a considerable number of pictures by Giacomo Nani (1698-1770), as well as some by Domenico Maria Sani (1690-1773), who occasionally painted still lifes of hunting subjects and worked under the express direction of the Queen. In the extensive inventories of her collections are to be found other canvases of French and Italian origin, with flowers and similar images.[109]

Many paintings by Giacomo Nani, all small in scale, entered the Royal Collection in the first half of the eighteenth century. The palace of Riofrío conserves a series of twenty four canvases which belonged to Elizabeth. In this curious series of still lifes, Nani reveals himself to be a painter of

99 Sánchez Cantón, 1959-1960; Urrea Fernández, 1979-1981.

100 Guinard, 1956.

101 Marañón, 1953.

102 Bru Romo, 1971; Bédat, 1989.

103 Lafuente Ferrari, 1944; Gállego, 1976.

104 Caveda, 1867; Bédat, 1989.

105 Urrea Fernández, 1979-1981.

106 Fontaine, 1909.

107 Armstrong, 1892; Taxonera, 1943; Lavalle-Cobo, 2002.

108 Luna, 1973.

109 *Inventarios reales*, 1746; Urrea Fernández, 1977; La Granja de San Ildefonso, 2000.

a rather dry style, betraying none of the superficial, ostentatious decorative qualities of his mentor, Gasparo López (died c.1732). The latter, known as 'Gasparino', was of possible Spanish ascendancy and was well known in Neapolitan circles. Although Nani followed closely the ideals of his master, he was not able to give as effective expression to background landscapes, nor had he the same sense of creative delight. On the contrary, he tended to be more archaic and sometimes abrupt and hasty, although he did possess a powerful palette based on intense colours with gentle shading. An attenuated tenebrism is evident in his play of light and shade, as is a sense of objectivity in his manner of presenting objects. These methods, together with a tendency to simplify the elements of the picture with a certain coarseness, means that the objects which appear before the spectator seem more precise, conveying a direct, if cold, impression which is not altogether agreeable. His approach displays in some cases a certain sobriety which has led to his being classified, not entirely accurately, as the immediate predecessor, both in time and space, of Meléndez. Indeed, his pictures may have influenced court painters, and probably did contribute to some extent to Meléndez's inclination towards the genre. They might well have met in Naples, then governed by Charles VII, the monarch who would later become Charles III of Spain.

Aspects of the Reign of Charles III

During the reign of this king there occurred a decisive time of 'enlightened despotism', the fruit of various foreign influences on Spanish traditions which coincided with the period when ideological tendencies from the other side of the Pyrenees were at their most influential within the Iberian Peninsula.[110] These trends were assimilated by numerous members of the governing élite, the nobles, and the nascent bourgeoisie, which was beginning to assert itself, but not by the vast majority of society, which remained wedded to conservative principles, as if mere spectators viewing the reforms which would transform their country. It is not surprising, therefore, that in the future this almost immovable sector of society would be profoundly affected by the impact of the French Revolution, which alerted its various groups and led them to dig in deeper in their incalcitrance.

Gradually, as in the rest of Europe, a prosperous bourgeoisie flourished and began to assert its own influence in the transformation of artistic sensibility. Although this was more evident in Madrid than in the provinces, in various places in Spain there were groups from this class who were more or less interested in intellectual and aesthetic questions. The church monopoly began to give way, bourgeois portraits began to appear, and, in academic circles, classical, historical, and mythological themes were introduced. At the same time, the key motifs and popular themes of the genre began to develop, and in the theatre and in prose fiction a tendency to treat issues of daily life emerged, with more 'plebeian' representations of the lifestyle and diversions of the upper classes, although still preserving a sense of their dignity. During the splendid second half of the eighteenth century, Spain seemed to be working towards her due place in the European artistic panorama. Academies contributed to the education of

110 Domínguez Ortiz, 1976.

many students, the number of which increased with the passing years and, as a consequence, Spanish painters, who had always been closely associated with religious art, became familiar with the mythological, allegorical, and historical themes that often formed the basis of court commissions.

Regarding the decoration of royal palaces, and particularly those in Madrid, it should be noted that at the beginning of his reign, Charles III called to the court two of the most distinguished figures in European painting: Gian Battista Tiepolo[111] and Antón Rafael Mengs,[112] whose work was decisive in the evolution of Spanish painting, constituting as it did the foreign contribution which would finally place Spain squarely on the European international scene.

When the Venetian Tiepolo (died 1770) arrived in the Iberian Peninsula in 1762 he was already of advanced years[113] but was still well able, with the help of his sons, to execute some of his greatest masterpieces, especially the frescoes of the Royal Palace in Madrid and an important series of canvases. His style – the apotheosis of the monumental, grandiloquence of the Baroque, but infused with Italian elegance – was admired, although not sufficiently, as it happened to coincide with the awakening of neoclassicism. On the other hand, Mengs (died 1779) – a German artist, born in Bohemia, who established himself in Madrid in 1761, and whose pictures, of a formal and extraordinarily rigorous classicism, were the very incarnation of this new devotion towards ancient times – was exhalted as a genius and his views were decisive in the direction of the San Fernando Academy, which would flounder under severely classicist artistic dogma.[114]

Mengs painted the ceilings of the Royal Palace and executed a considerable number of portraits, always with care and precision, and with a cold finish which resembled enamel but retained a certain grace in the positioning of male figures and the coquettishness of the females. His style exerted enormous influence over painters of the final third of the century, including those who had trained under the Italianate Rococo spirit of Giaquinto and Tiepolo.

As a result of these complex aesthetic convergences, the revitalization of Spanish painting was consolidated following the decade 1760-1770, even before the death of Tiepolo. Thus, the reappearance of a lost artistic originality was not exclusively the result of the education of various generations. It coincided with, and was conditioned by, contacts with Italy and France, which became ever closer under the rule of Charles III. One can state with certainty that the only opposition to this national style came from two directions: the traditional importance of homegrown tendencies in their most recent manifestation, and recourse to foreign sources. Both these phenomena were not only compatible, but necessary. Spanish art ought not to be reduced to its relations with Europe, since the importance of a formal exchange of ideas in both general and specifically artistic terms should be recognised along with the prevailing artistic character of each cultural realm.[115]

Concerning Luis Meléndez

With the accession of Charles III to the Spanish throne, interest in still life painting must have grown, and this would have intensified through contacts with Naples.

111 Pedrocco, 2002.

112 Sánchez Cantón, 1929; Roettgen, 1999.

113 Morassi, 1962; Palucchini, 1968.

114 Salas and Águeda, 1980; Luna, 1980; Águeda Villar, 1981.

115 Réau, 1971.

Fig. 31: Attributed to Luis Meléndez, *Still Life with Bowl of Figs, Plate of Strawberries and Peaches*
Oil on canvas, 42 x 67,5 cm
Private collection

Fig. 32: Attributed to Luis Meléndez, *Still Life with Bowl of Plums, Peaches and a Piece of Watermelon*
Oil on canvas, 42 x 67,5 cm
Private collection

The figure of Meléndez is closely linked to Naples, not only because this was the place of his birth — a circumstance whose importance is difficult to judge beyond a possible sense of nostalgia which led him to return there when his position in Madrid became untenable — but also because of its influence on his formative years as a still life painter. Moreover, his work is rigorously contempor- -aneous with the reign of the illustrious monarch under whose aegis he painted the major series of canvases which belong to the Prado Museum and form part of the National Patrimony, and were destined to be left to his son, the Prince of Asturias and future Charles IV.[116]

Luis Meléndez (figs 31, 32) was born in Naples in 1716 and, although he immediately moved with his parents to the Iberian Peninsula, his family background, as the son of a painter who had lived in Southern Italy, was enriched with Neapolitan influences. The importance of these origins was doubtless reinforced when, towards the end of the 1740s, he returned to Naples for some time to paint. Although he took as a point of departure the works of Nani and Caro,

which were characterised by a rich palette of colours, decorative magnificence, and a superficial view of the objects concerned, Meléndez adopted a rigorous approach to composition, tending towards formal monumentalism and precise detail.[117] These features are highly personal and they create the effect of a hyperrealism, at once technically perfect and endowed with a fascinating expressiveness which evokes the sense of mystery of Spanish seventeenth century still life painting yet also conveys a profane spirit. The magic of Meléndez is based on his single, coherent vision of the intrinsic, tangible qualities of the inanimate objects he paints and in the skill with which he represents their surroundings. Thus, he always used carefully calculated lighting effects, seemingly implacable but actually intended to highlight the varying textures and volumes, rather than a gentle or diffused light, which would tend towards the dissolution of form and line.

At any rate, the true range of influences which can be seen in the *oeuvre* of this formidable painter of still lifes are not easily identified, despite the fact that there has been

116 Luna, 1992.

117 Prota-Giurleo, 1953; Causa, 1961; Lotu, 1961; Naples, 1964; Spinosa, 1979.

Fig. 33: Attributed to Giovanni Battista Crescenzi,
Still Life with Flowers, Fruit and Vegetables
Oil on canvas, 104,8 x 139,7 cm
Raleigh (North Carolina), North Carolina Museum of Art

Fig. 34: Giuseppe Recco,
Still Life with a Black Servant
Oil on canvas, 176 x 255 cm
Seville, Fundación Casa Ducal de Medinaceli

much speculation about Neapolitan examples of the genre which he may have known either in Spain or in Italy. What did he see? What aspects particularly interested him and captivated him? Which, of all the motifs and features of the Italian school of painting, did he choose to place in the melting pot of his own personality in order to form so finished, coherent and distinctive a language of painting? Taking into account the four recently-discovered pictures, which are signed by him and dated 1750 – that is to say, to the time of his Italian sojourn[118] – but still reveal hesitancy in the choice of a direction to follow, and bearing in mind his later development – from the miniatures in choral books in the Royal Chapel to the series of still lifes done from the beginning of the 1770s to the end of the 1780s – the view which emerges is one of numerous influences which he would later fuse, at first with hesitation and later with greater confidence, in his particular, clearly-structured technique.

As a result, it is not surprising that in his career one can seen a preference for the early principles of the Caravaggio circle in Rome –

painters such as the Pensionante del Saraceni (first half of the seventeenth century), Tommaso Salini (c.1575-1625), Giovanni Battista Crescenzi (1577-1635), (fig. 33), Pietro Paolo Bonzi (c.1576-1636), Agostino Verrocchi (dated 1619-1636) and others – from the beginning of the seventeenth century, moving towards the ideas underpinning the work of the Neapolitan Luca Forte (c.1605 – c.1670) and that unusual artist with a naturalist style, Giovanni Quinsa (mid seventeenth century). Meléndez is also not unfamiliar with the tradition, also from Neapolitan circles, of Tommaso Realfonso, known as Masillo (c.1677-after 1745), although he deals with themes with an expressiveness and technique evidently superior to him. Therefore, reviewing the circumstances and the visible resemblances with Giovan Battista Recco (1615?-before 1660); the aforementioned Giuseppe Recco (1634-1695) (fig. 34); Andrea Belvedere (c.1652-1732); Giuseppe Ruoppolo (c.1630-1710) (fig. 35); Paolo Porpora (1617-1673) (fig. 36); and even the mysterious Francisco della Quosta (or Questa), probably a Spaniard

118 Cottino, 2000.

named Cuesta (c.1639-1723) (fig. 37) and seemingly a student of Ruoppolo's – reviewing the work of these, it may be true that, at one time or another, they offered Meléndez concrete examples to follow. Nevertheless, one can see clearly the extent to which he distinguished himself from their theatricality in order to concentrate on a more austere style which is close, if not exactly similar, to the suggestive indulgence of the treatment of immediate reality evident in Gaspare Traversi (early eighteenth century-1769). This is particularly evident when he displays his unusual tendency towards a sort of anti-Baroque (not, of course, of neoclassical origin), in which he played down pomposity and ceremony in the interests of developing the principles of a more convincing vision of daily life and a greater faithfulness to the evidence of its immediacy, hence renouncing excesses and extravagances. Other possible models which should be taken into account – though they are suggestions without substantiation – are the works of Giacomo Ceruti (1698-1767) (fig. 38) in Lombardy, and Carlo Magini

Fig. 37: Francesco della Quosta, *Still Life with Vegetables, Hoe and a Landscape with Peasant and a Carthorse*
Oil on canvas, 100 x 145 cm
Madrid, private collection

Fig. 35: Giuseppe Ruoppolo,
Kitchen Still Life
Oil on canvas, 78 x 151 cm
Madrid, Prado Museum, no. 1990

Fig. 38: Giacomo Ceruti, *Still Life with Pewter Plate, Knife, Bread, Meat, Nuts, Glass and Jug*
Oil on paper on canvas, 32 x 45 cm
Private collection

Fig. 36: Paolo Porpora,
Still Life with Vase, Flowers and Fruit
Oil on canvas, 148 x 113 cm
Naples, Museo Nazionale di Capodimonte

Fig. 39: Giovanni Stanchi, *Still Life with Watermelons, Pears and Bowl of Fruit in a Landscape*
Oil on canvas, 135 x 98 cm
Monaco, private collection

Fig. 40: Ubaldo Gandolfi,
Still Life with Bottle, Bread and Cheese
Oil on canvas, 38 x 48 cm
Bergamo, private collection

(1720-1806) in the Po Valley, given their influence beyond their own particular region.

With all that has been said above, there is no need to insist on other evidence of similarities, convergences, and possible or even probable relations in the themes and ideas which Meléndez is at pains to sketch into his artistic expression. He thus incorporated the varied succession of impressions gained from contemplating, studying and absorbing the attitudes, talents and formal characteristics of the works which his colleagues, in the space of a century and a half, completed in Italy and which he was able to see. A crucial case can be made for the works of Evaristo Baschenis (1617-1677) from Bergamo; Filippo d'Angeli or Liagno, better known as Filippo Napoletano (c.1587-1629); Bartolomeo Bimbi (1648-1729); Simone del Tintore (1630-1708); or Cristoforo Munari (1667-1720); all from the Alpine and Tuscan areas of northern of Italy.

Nor should one forget the polished, splendid advances of art in Baroque Rome, with all its cosmopolitan magnificence and exuberance. These are clearly evident in the works of Giovanni Stanchi (1608-after 1673) (fig. 39); Michelangelo Pace, nicknamed 'Michelangelo of the Campidoglio' (1610?-1670?); perhaps Abraham Brueghel (1631-1697); certainly Christian Berentz (1658-1722); Pietro Navarra (end seventeenth century-beginning eighteenth century); and Franz Werner von Tamm, who was known as 'Monsieur Daprait' (1658-1724). In analogous terms the works of later masters reveal similarities with Meléndez and it is not surprising that, for one reason or another, they may have lodged in his imagination, as is the case with Ubaldo Gandolfi (1711-1776) (fig. 40), to cite just one artist who clearly stands out.

With all this, in Western Europe, theory and practice were intimately linked during the eighteenth century, and whoever wished to offer an innovative view of the world could draw upon the abundant bibliography in existence, since, by way of an introduction to the area, the famous Abate Pluche was widely read in cultured circles. His treatise on nature, which underlined divine knowledge by distinguishing the particular characteristics of objects one from another, was especially well consulted. At the same time, interest grew in botany and the classification of fruits and plants; as a result, the writings of Linneo and Buffon were a great success on their publication. It is reasonable to assume that there were certain ideas, perhaps with some doctrinal import, although not necessarily explicitly taught as such, which influenced both Meléndez and other artists in their employment of precise forms in the representation of phenomena, effects, and protagonists from nature, even if for decorative ends.[119]

Still Life in France

When one also observes the wide and eloquent panorama of French painting at the end of the seventeenth century and throughout the eighteenth century – the final years of the reign of Louis XIV (died 1715), the regency (1715-1723), the era of Louis XV (1723-1774) and that of Louis XVI (1774/1789-1793) – one becomes aware of an incredibly superb flowering of formidable artistic talent and wonderful creativity which had little or no impact in Spain, and particularly on Meléndez. Nevertheless, and more due to parallel development than a convergence of influences, a knowledge of particular topics or an attachment to certain criteria, one can see some similarities and peculiar features, perhaps because both the Spaniard and many French artists conserved a common admiration for the successes of a prestigious recent past. The seventeenth century's most significant and accomplished representatives had achieved considerable elegance and undeniable power in the variety and technical characteristics of their work. Moreover, there is an underlying tendency towards austerity and classicism manifest throughout the whole century on the other side of the Pyrenees, in, for instance, historical paintings and some landscapes, which are distanced from any sense of pomp and magnificence. They are centred, rather, on a more rigorous analytical, almost contemplative, view which displays a preference for intimacy. One can also see this in the approach to still life cultivated by some artists, simply because there existed influential figures and lesser clients with these tastes.

Some pictures by Pierre-Nicolas Huilliot (1647-1751) were on occasion determined by such principles, even given the pomposity which frequently dominated his work. The same may be said of Guillaume-Thomas-Raphaël Taraval (1701-1750), who sometimes surprises with his notably serene and polished pictorial anecdotes, and even André Bouys (1656-1740), whose compositions are generally sober when they do not involve human figures, although the objects which he combines belong to different, economically-prosperous social levels.

In clear opposition to this we find the compositions of Nicolas de Largilliere (1656-1746), Alexandre-François Desportes (1661-1743), and Jean Baptiste Oudry (1686-1755) (fig. 41), for whom the theatricality of portraiture – particularly in the case of the first and third, who were even for a time master and student – was complemented, whether for the sake of refinement or creativity, by details from the wide spectrum of *nature morte*. They also included as motifs

119 Pluche, 1732; Monet, 1907.

Fig. 41: Jean-Baptiste Oudry,
Still Life with Sugar Loaf
Oil on canvas, 122 x 65 cm
Besançon, Musée des Beaux-Arts et d'Archéologie

Fig. 42: Jean-Baptiste-Siméon Chardin,
Still Life with Fruit and a Silver Cup
Oil on canvas, 30 x 42 cm
Boston, Museum of Fine Arts

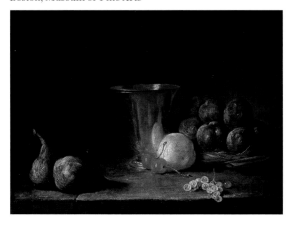

from architecture, hunting, interior décor, and even whimsical accessories, in order to emphasise the status of their eminent clientele. That did not prevent them from producing wonderful paintings outside the still life genre, as one can see from their works in collections and museums – Largilliere becoming famous for his portraits and Oudry for hunting scenes and depictions of animals and landscapes.

However, over and above these artists and many others yet to be mentioned, one particular figure stands out, not just in French still life painting of the eighteenth century, but across all the centuries, for the energy and individuality of his canvases: Jean-Baptiste-Siméon Chardin (1699-1779) (fig. 42). Given their contemporaneity – the Frenchman was born seventeen years before the Spaniard and died but a year before him – as well as interest in a common genre and mutual artistic idiom, Meléndez has consistently been compared to Chardin, despite the absence of aesthetic and technical links between them, and irrespective of the differing mental and expressive qualities of their work. Chardin is the more varied in his use of themes and the scale of his works, and in matters of technique and lyrical inspiration. On the other hand, Meléndez is more repetitive, forceful, and rooted in everyday reality, in contrast to the refinements of the Parisian. One should not forget that Chardin entered the Academy at the age of twenty nine and exhibited pictures on various themes in the salons, breaking the mould and renewing outmoded forms thanks to his particular approach to composition. The subtlety and strength of his palette and the richness of his visual resources are marshalled in the service of an especially careful expression of the profoundly poetic grandeur of everyday life in all its guises.

There are other masters worthy of mention, to the extent that they work in a manner not all that distant from certain features of Meléndez's work – even if one cannot speak of concrete links or influence, but only of a common point of view and shared tendency towards the expression of an individual realism. The elegantly decorative Thomas-Germain Duvivier (1735-1814); that most original cultivator of fantasy drawn out of reality, Henri-Horace Roland de la Porte (1725-1793); the great follower of Chardin, Nicolas-Henri Jeaurat de Bertry (1728-1796) (fig. 43); the supremely eclectic and surprisingly versatile Michel-Honoré Bounieu (1740-1814); the varied, prudent, sensitive and admirable Jean-Etienne Liotard (1702-1789) (fig. 44); all of whose work culminates in the fascinating, delicately explicit style of Anne Vallayer-Coster (1744-1818) (figs 45 and 46), the most famous painter of still life in the whole of the eighteenth century. After such significant figures, one might mention certain other personalities of worth whose artistic production and spirit are all the more meretricious when taken as a whole, thus highlighting their formal discoveries and decorative profundity: Louis Tessier (c.1719-1781), Jean-Jacques Bachelier (1724-1806), Piat-Joseph Sauvage (1744-1818), and Antoine Marcenay de Ghuy (1724-1811). Similarly, it is justifiable to include here various artists from the provincial scene who followed the dominant trends coming from Paris: amongst them are Dominique Pergaut (1729-1808) in Lorraine; Claude-Joseph Fraichot (1732-1803) and Fançois Vispré (c.1730-c.1790) from Franche-Comté; and Lié-Louis Perin Salbreux (1753-1817) from Reims, with whom one can close this brief survey which, for reasons of space, must omit certain other eloquent talents worthy of mention along side their distinguished colleagues.[120]

Fig. 43: Nicolas-Henri Jeaurat de Bertry, *Still Life with Kitchen Utensils*, 1756
Oil on canvas, 129 x 161 cm
Paris, École Nationale Supérieure des Beaux-Arts

Fig. 44: Jean-Etienne Liotard, *Still Life with Pears, Figs, Plums, Bread Roll, and a Knife on a Table*, 1782
Pastel on canvas, 33 x 38 cm
Geneva, Musée d'Art et d'Histoire

120 Faré, 1976.

Fig. 45: Anne Vallayer-Coster, *A Kitchen Table*
Oil on panel, 28 x 33 cm
Berlin, Staatliche Museen zu
Berlin, Gemäldegalerie

Fig. 46: Anne Vallayer-Coster,
Still Life with a Basket of Plums, 1769
Oil on canvas, 38 x 46,2 cm
Cleveland (Ohio), The Cleveland Museum of Art

Spain: Mariano Nani and Luis Paret

Returning again to the particular atmosphere of eighteenth century Spain, so different from that of France, one must bear in mind that numerous artists singled out Mariano Nani (c.1725-1804) as a significant presence. He arrived in the Iberian Peninsula to work as a painter at the Buen Retiro Porcelain Workshop and was the first painter of still lifes to be admitted to the San Fernando Royal Academy as an honorary member. He painted fabric designs for the Santa Barbara workshop,[121] generally hunting scenes with a strong Flemish influence, and he did various still lifes for the future Queen María Luisa. His style evolved from the naturalist school of his father, Giacomo, and then changed, probably as a result of his studies of collections of Flemish art at the Madrid Court.[122] In his artistic expression — which is at times very intense, with lively contrasts — one can see the stamp of painters like Snyders, Fyt, and Paul de Vos. In some cases, he used a less energetic decorative style, more of French inspiration, with the colder colour palette characteristic of the eighteenth century, rich in greens and greys and depicting refined and luminous landscapes in the background. This style came more from the Rococo spirit of courtly life than from contact with painters across the Pyrenees. His technique, so exact and detailed, was a combination of Nordic influences and Neapolitan daily life, with some elements of *trompe l'oeil*, which reveal his considerable skill.

One could write much about the Madrid artist, Luis Paret y Alcázar (1746-1799) (fig. 47), a fascinating painter and the undisputed master of the most exquisite refinements of Rococo.[123] His contribution to still life painting has not been extensively studied and, with the exception of two pictures currently in the Prado Museum and a few which exist in private collections, little is known about him. The floral motifs and beautiful objects which often appear in his religious pictures or in his elegant party

121 Held, 1971; Urrea Fernández, 1977.

122 Díaz Padrón, 1975.

123 Luna, 1984; Bilbao, 1991-1992.

scenes are confined to hidden corners, but they are always fully integrated, giving a sense of joy and sumptuousness to his entire output. Paret developed harmonious colour contrasts, playing with warm and cold tones with an exemplary technical mastery, applying the paint with skilful brushstrokes and creating effects of light on gems, leaves, petals, porcelain, or glass. Likewise, his use of light and shade conveys an apparently effortless verisimilitude in the depiction of enamel, pearls, and other materials. More versed in literature than was usual, Paret seems to have endowed his floral arrangements with a concealed symbolism in which the arcane language of flowers plays a principal role.[124] His works evoke the French style, and although this has often been said with reference to his multifaceted compositions,[125] his delightful floral motifs

Fig. 47: Luis Paret y Alcázar,
Bouquet of Flowers
Oil on canvas, 39 x 37 cm
Madrid, Prado Museum, no. 1042

have been singled out by some comparative critics[126] as similar in certain details to the above-mentioned Parisian, Anne Vallayer-Coster and to works by Michel-Nicholas Micheux (1679-1733).[127] Nor should one forget his beautiful plates of plants, flowers, and birds, drawn with such care that they are illustrations of great interest, even in the field of Natural Science.

The Importance of Madrid

Along with these two painters, both reputed masters of Rococo, there were many others who stood out for their great creativity. A considerable number of them arrived in Madrid from remote corners of the peninsula, drawn by the prestige of the court, important commissions, and the possibility of contact with other colleagues, as well as the seductiveness of the capital itself. Their sojourn there was to be decisive for the development of the Spanish school. Cándido García Romeral (died 1783), who specialised in flower painting, was elected an honorary member of the San Fernando Academy in 1765. The Majorcan Cristóbal Vilella (died 1803) studied in that same Madrid institution and worked with Mengs. He painted flowers and plants and depicted marvellous marine motifs, such as fish, shells, snails, etc. He travelled in Italy, passing through Naples and other cities. He was also a naturalist and, seemingly, a taxidermist. Lorenzo Marín is a little-known painter; born in Madrid, he collaborated as a flower illustrator for *Flora española*, published between 1762 and 1784.[128] In 1772, José Garcés (died c.1802) possibly from Valencia, entered the San Fernando Academy as an honorary member. One of his

124 Hait, 1913.

125 Baticle, 1966.

126 Luna, 1984.

127 Faré, 1976.

128 Cavestany, 1936-1940.

floral arrangements is of excellent quality and admirable composition, with a delicate palette made up of rich, transparent tones.[129] As a work, it has a traditional air and seems to be related to French examples of the period of transition from the seventeenth to the eighteenth century.[130] In his youth, he may have worked in the Alcora workshop, judging by the list of painters who contributed designs to its ceramics. Another painter with an unknown biography is Ramón Castellanos, named an honorary academician in 1774. His only known works are two baskets of fruit which he presented to the Academy on his admission. Their delicate execution and excellent quality reveal a solid technical foundation; they are closer to the French school than the Neapolitan, which seemed to dominate Spanish aesthetics of the time.[131]

Painters of the Royal Tapestry Workshop

During these years, the Santa Barbara Royal Tapestry Workshop, under the expert direction of Mengs,[132] undertook designs for the decoration of palaces. Hunting motifs and scenes of popular imagery were the most frequent themes for these marvellous tapestries, which sometimes contained vary varied still lifes. Artists like the earlier-mentioned Mariano Nani, or another Italian, Antonio Barbazza, or the Madrid painter José del Castillo (1737-1793) made designs which were authentic still lifes, evoking the Flemish works so common in royal residences. Castillo was especially distinguished since his personal sources of inspiration, which he probably knew from engravings, were often of French origin.[133] His still lifes, like the details which appear in several of his works,

are full of popular charm and precision in the depiction of everyday scenes. They reveal the extent to which he had assimilated the key themes prevailing in contemporary Europe and they stand out for their elegant, decorative representation of reality, which tends to monumentality but is still realistic. Similar to Castillo was Andrés Ginés de Aguirre (1727-?), a skilful designer of tapestries, some of whose creations can be included in the category of still life.[134] He painted background landscapes with, in the foreground, ceramics, kitchen utensils, arms or hunting motifs, and sometimes also dogs. These were the real subjects, as there was a complete absence of figures or architectural details.

Other artists who toiled in the same workshop included the Bayeus, the González Velázquez, Guillermo Anglois, and Tellez, amongst others. The same variety of motifs and objects appear in their compositions, and are a testament to their ability to handle the standard themes of still life painting, although details are necessarily subordinated to the scenes of a popular and everyday character which prevailed in the patterns. These would later be passed to the craftsmen to be woven.[135]

One should mention here Mariano Salvador Maella (1739-1819), an important court painter who stressed the diversity of objects in still lifes in order to convey a greater sense of verisimilitude in the overall arrangement.[136] He excelled in his treatment of flowers, although he was not necessarily especially gifted at still life; he can thus be regarded as a secondary practitioner of the genre, since he used its motifs to fill minor areas of his compositions.

129 Cavestany, 1936-1940; Pérez Sánchez, 1983-1984.

130 Faré, 1974.

131 Cavestany, 1936-1940; Pérez Sánchez, 1983-1984.

132 Held, 1971.

133 Sambricio, 1958.

134 Held, 1971.

135 Held, 1971.

136 Alcolea, 1967; Junquera de Vega, 1973-1974; Morales y Marín, 1996.

Juan Batista Romero and José López Enguídanos

Returning to still life in the strict sense of the term, there are numerous other painters who have attracted the attention of researchers and others studying the development of Spanish art. Talents from the provinces were always attracted to the court, and Valencia contributed an important number.[137] Of particular interest is Juan Bautista Romero (1756-after 1802) (figs 48, 49, and 50), about whom it is difficult to find information. The frequently high quality of his works, in spite of their naivety, is notable, as is his tendency towards perfectionism (which sometimes prevails over his aesthetic sense) and the graceful balance of his flower paintings and still lifes proper.[138] A certain mastery in exclusively floral works is evident, with echoes of French tendencies from several years earlier. His most notable qualities are careful composition, colour harmony, and a fresh yet precise technique. He also attempted to convey the texture of materials in order to heighten the sense of authenticity – in the delicacy of the petals, the lightness of the tendrils and the luminosity of the glass – resulting in agreeable effects which are pleasant to the eye. The groupings of flowers seem to be animated by a finely balanced use of light

Fig. 48: Juan Bautista Romero,
Basket of Fruit, 1800
Oil on canvas, 81 x 62,5 cm
Madrid, Patrimonio Nacional

Fig. 49: Juan Bautista Romero, *Flower Piece*, 1796
Oil on canvas, 55 x 37 cm
Madrid, Real Academia de Bellas
Artes de San Fernando

137 Aldana Fernández, 1970.

138 Cavestany, 1936-1940;
Aldana Fernández, 1970;
Pérez Sánchez, 1983-1984;
Luna, 1984.

Fig. 50: Juan Bautista Romero, *Still Life with Strawberries and Chocolate*, c.1775-1790
Oil on canvas, 44,1 x 61,6 cm
Raleigh (North Carolina),
North Carolina Museum of Art

and shade, which becomes the agent for creating contrasts between opacity and transparency. His still lifes also reveal some details which recall a combination of inspirational sources in Spanish art, modified by a more distant, deliberate echo of some aspects of eighteenth century French painting. However, he seems to understand the powerful sense of definition and precision in Meléndez's work, paying homage to his perfection whilst, at the same time, striving for a more decorative and delicate formulation.

The Valencian, José López Enguídanos (1760-1812), a painter and engraver,[139] is much less sensitive to the genre than Romero. Like the latter, he moved to Madrid and there is evidence that he studied at the San Fernando Academy. Despite this prestigious training, his paintings suffer from an undisguised mediocrity, even if he was an able painter of still lifes and knew Meléndez, whose works he tried in some cases to imitate. Critics reproach him for the hardness of his profiles, his lack of subtlety, and a disagreeable rigidity, all of which stems from his inability

to adapt to the neoclassical techniques, more oriented towards diversity and precision in the use of colour, which prevailed at that time. His manner of expressing the essential character of the objects he depicted is, to a degree, reminiscent of Flemish painting, which he probably saw in the Royal Collection, and of Mariano Nani, where such effects are also evident. Another, relatively unknown, painter is Manuel Muñoz de Ugena, who worked in the Madrid court, depicting flowers, festoons, and friezes for palace decorations in the final years of the reign of Charles III and then under Charles IV.[140] He also did designs of motifs for marquetry.[141]

In Andalusia, on the other hand, few really good painters emerged. In Cordoba, Rafael Hidalgo y Vázquez was known for his quill and ink drawings of *mesas revueltas* [sundry collections of objects], rather in the manner of *trompe l'oeil* from earlier in the century. José Pérez Ruano (died 1810), also a Cordoban, did similar pictures. He was popular both within and beyond Spain as, according to Ramírez de Arellano, 'his *mesas revueltas* were notable and foreigners paid high prices for them'.[142]

In Galicia, or more precisely in Santiago de Compostela in the final third of the eighteenth century, there worked a painter who is of some interest – Ramón Torres – although little by his hand has so far been discovered. His poor and rather old-fashioned compositions look more to the past than to the future. The two works which we have by him, signed and dated 1729, reflect a clear dependence on the previous century; they are technically mediocre, expressively bland, and both lack any of the necessary sparkle to lift them beyond a purely decorative role.

139 Gallego, 1979.
140 Junquera y Mato, 1979.
141 Luna, 1984.
142 Cavestany, 1936-1940.

Still Life and Flower Painting in the Second Half of the Eighteenth Century

The important role played by Valencia in the revitalization of Spanish painting requires special attention.[143] In 1754 a temporary academy, Santa Barbara, was created and eleven years later a preparatory committee was charged with the foundation of a royal academy, which was inaugurated in 1768 with monarchical patronage under the name of the San Carlos Royal Academy. It would be one of the most creative in the peninsula after that of San Fernando in Madrid.[144] The Valencia academy introduced important talents into the Spanish school, particularly in the area of painting, since many of her young students moved to Madrid, contributing to the modernization of the very idea of painting. Some of the artists cited above were originally from Valenica, and there are many others of the period who should be mentioned, most especially Vicente López, Goya's successor in the most important artistic post at the Madrid court, who worked mainly in the first half of the nineteenth century.[145]

Indeed, Valencia was especially strong in studies of still life, sending excellent painters not only to the court, but also to the San Carlos Academy, mostly to the department known as the Salon of Flowers and Ornamentation, set up in 1778. This type of painting was subordinate to the grand style, but had the fundamental aim of facilitating the prosperous silk industry with new compositions and designs. This salon trained various brilliant artists who were characterised by their irreproachable quality and promising future. Proof of this is that, although in 1784 the department was considered secondary, it later acquired the same standing as the other divisions of the Academy.[146]

The style of Félix Lorente (1712-1787) was closely linked to seventeenth century traditions. Specializing in still life and flower painting, although he also did religious works, he entered the San Carlos Academy in 1777. One can see similarities between his work and that of Meléndez, so much so that in one of his more uncommon still lifes, with modest objects from daily life, there is a precise and detailed technique which surprises the spectator in its expressiveness, its convincing interpretation of the textures of the objects, and the natural use of colour, characteristic of his colleagues in this regard. Although there were many other still life painters, their works have not survived to the present day. There is more information available on artists dedicated to flower painting, since the San Carlos Academy has retained documents as well as works on both paper and canvas. This group of artists was autonomous and possessed a distinctive ethos, although they never fully kept pace with the changes of modernization. They created works of considerable quality, in a luminous and agreeable style, imbued with an attractive bourgeois air that reflects nineteenth century aesthetic tastes without radical transformation or violent upheaval.

At that time many painters worked at the Academy, a practice which continued with successive generations.[147] One should mention names such as Aguilar, Baset, Bru, Burgos, Calado, Carrá, Cuevas, Esquerrer, Grifol, Medina del Pomar, Navarro, Pascual, Pompey, the Romás, Rosell, Soto, and Vivó. During the final years of the eighteenth

143 Alchali, 1897; Orellana, 1967.

144 Garín and Ortiz de Taranco, 1945.

145 Lozoya, 1943; Morales y Marín, 1979.

146 Aldana Fernández, 1970.

147 Cavestany, 1936-1940; Aldana Fernández, 1970.

Fig. 51: Josep Ferrer, *Vase with Flowers*, 1780
Oil on board, 27 x 35 cm
Barcelona, Museu de la Reial Acadèmia
Catalana de Bellas Artes de Sant Jordi

Fig. 52: Benito Espinós, *Vase of Flowers*
Oil on panel, 86 x 57 cm
Norfolk (Virginia), Chrysler Museum of Art

century, a few Valencians and some painters from other provinces painted there. Amongst these, those who stand out are Ferrer (fig. 51), Senté, Colechà, Zapata and Espinós. Because of their mastery and age, they were the leaders of the group and directed many of the Academy's activities.

Benito Espinós (1784-1818) (figs 52, 53, and 54) merits greater attention in this singular pleiad due to the number of his works, their exquisite quality, and his decisive role as director of studies from 1784 to 1815.[148] His pictures were varied and some of his works have about them an unmistakable air of the seventeenth century. He embellished his religious, mythological, and genre paintings with floral garlands, doubtless inspired by Flemish and Dutch works of similar type.[149] He often included details of classical elements towards the bottom of his paintings, which reflected his academic training. The general tone is joyful and festive, and there is an agreeable lightness typical of the eighteenth century. His multi-coloured garlands and large vases, arranged with a classical touch, mark a resemblance to similar French works,[150] although his creations are more traditional than those from the other side of the Pyrenees. In all his compositions, colour and the play of light and shade dominate, revealing a delicate sensibility and refined taste. Espinós also knew how to pass these attributes on to his best students. One of his contemporaries, Josep Ferrer (1746-1815), managed to combine a love of detail with a tendency

148 Aldana Fernández, 1968.

149 Warner, 1975;
Segal, 1982.

150 Faré, 1976.

Fig. 53: Benito Espinós
Flower Piece
Oil on panel, 60 x 42 cm
Madrid, Prado Museum, no. 4293

Fig. 54: Benito Espinós
Vase of Flowers
Oil on panel, 86 x 57 cm
Valencia, Museo de Bellas Artes

towards the more classical compositions of the seventeenth century; he followed Arellano and his contemporaries in charmingly lively, chromatic interpretations, adding to the advances of the eighteenth century, and allowing one to see a measure of the elegance and refinement of Rococo in his more decorative and international creations. He may have acquired this skill from studying engravings in this style, as was often the case in European workshops.[151] José Antonio Zapata (1763-1837) also formed part of this original group, and he directed the Academy from 1815 until his death. He was one of Valencia's most distinguished

flower painters. His work is wide-ranging and includes religious and historical themes, although he became famous for harmonious paintings and drawings in his speciality genre.[152]

The next generation, which painted in the first part of the nineteenth century, was characterised by a clearly eighteenth century spirit, and it was not in vain that it was trained under the masters already mentioned. It did not bring any significant new ideas, except for a few innovations which were more superficial than truly profound in the modern sense, but many of these painters were gifted with a certain originality.

151 Cavestany, 1936-1940; Ponz, 1947; Aldana Fernández, 1970; Pérez Sánchez, 1983-1984.

152 Aldana Fernández, 1970.

Fig. 55: Francisco Millán,
Still Life with Pears
Oil on canvas, 83 x 61 cm
Norfolk (Virginia), Chrysler Museum of Art

Fig. 56: Salvador Molet, *Flower Painting*
Oil on panel, 57 x 86 cm
Barcelona, Museu de la Reial Acadèmia
Catalana de Bellas Artes de Sant Jordi

Francisco Millán (c.1777-after 1837) (fig. 55) did delicate depictions of flowers and other fabric designs, and he also painted powerfully expressive still lifes, animal pictures and portraits.[153] Miguel Parra (1780-1846), who was known as the 'Vicente López of flower painting', was the author of portraits as well as the usual arrangements and drawings of flowers and some good-quality still lifes.[155] His *oeuvre* reveals a marked tendency for architectural backgrounds, or fragments of columns and pedestals, all done with great powers of observation and a highly developed decorative sense, which recalls French examples of the transition period from the eighteenth to the nineteenth century.[155] José Romá (1784-1847) belongs to the expressive school of Espinós and Parra. His paintings reveal the academic training of his formative years, and the taste of his clientele, both determined by the atmosphere of Valencia and its School.[156] Salvador Molet (1773-1836) (fig. 56), from Barcelona, joined the Valencian group in 1791. He moved to the city in order to specialise in floral themes, bringing his

experiences to Barcelona's La Lonja School some time later.[157] He was very prolific and can be classed as of the same status as his Valencian colleagues. His style is developed from that of Espinós and reveals his love of pomp and theatricality. His exquisite and intimate compositions, comparable in skill and precision with the latter's, are elegant and harmonious creations drawn with precision and painted with a refined use of colour. In the different phases of his development, one can see a sort of romanticism, touched by a relative severity, half way between the force of the Baroque and the sobriety of neoclassicism.

Another Catalan, also from Barcelona, was Francesc Lacoma y Fontanet (1784-1849) (fig. 57), who may be considered part of the group mentioned above, although he had no connection with Valencia.[158] He trained at Barcelona's La Lonja School of Drawing, moving to Paris in 1804 to perfect his style. There he experienced the apogee of Napoleonic imperialism and probably met David and other great masters, since he maintained relations with a nucleus of

153 Aldana Fernández, 1970.

154 Pérez Sánchez, 1983-1984.

155 Faré, 1976.

156 Aldana Fernández, 1970; Pérez Sánchez, 1983-1984.

157 Cavestany, 1936-1940; Gudiol, Alcolea, Cirlot, s/d; Subias Galter, 1951; Pérez Sánchez, 1983-1984.

158 Fontbona and Durá, 1999.

French, Belgian, and Dutch still life painters. His canvases reflect his strong, esoteric links with the work of Gérard van Spaendonck, Jan Frans van Dael, Christian van Pol, and Pierre-Joseph Redouté, who were fashionable in Paris.[159] His cold technique, resembling enamel, is evidence of his detailed knowledge of such painters, and his execution – meticulous and pictorial in the smallest of details – proves his mastery in this style. He painted still lifes and flower paintings of an excellent standard, and also portraits and other genres. Wholly integrated into Parisian life, the return of many paintings removed from the Iberian Peninsula during the French invasion is due to him. He died in Paris, where he spent the greater part of his creative life. One of his contemporaries was Gabriel Planella (c.1780-1850), a member of the famous Planella family of painters.

His canvases, especially those depicting landscapes and flowers, are in accord with the aesthetic of the nineteenth century and are evidence of his talent for Neapolitan and Flemish styles.[160] The peak of his career coincided with the reigns of Ferdinand VII and Isabella II.

There were also in Madrid various painters, born and educated in the eighteenth century, who continued to use archaic styles well into the nineteenth century.[161] One example is the Segovian Bartolomé Montalvo (1769-1846) (fig. 58), a disciple of Zacarías González Velázquez and student at the San Fernando Academy. His works, rather dry in technique but with a powerful use of colour, are fully within the still life genre and yet reveal his skill as a painter of landscape. He was evidently skilled in combining elements from eighteenth century tradition, and his works

Fig. 57: Francesc Lacoma y Fontanet,
Flower Piece, 1805
Oil on canvas, 116 x 90 cm
Barcelona, Museu de la Reial Acadèmia
Catalana de Bellas Artes de Sant Jordi, on loan
to Barcelona, Museu Nacional d'Art de Catalunya

Fig. 58: Bartolomé Montalvo,
Still Life with Game
Oil on panel, 55 x 72 cm
Madrid, Prado Museum, no. 4515

159 Faré, 1976.

160 Cavestany, 1936-1940.

161 Ossorio y Bernard, 1883-1884.

reveal a profound knowledge of Meléndez's aesthetic. Montalvo never reached the vital synthesis necessary to breathe new life into nineteenth century painting, whose future was clearly laid out in Goya's still lifes. It is obvious that he did not learn the magnificent lesson of that Aragonese master, possibly because he had either not seen his pictures or had not heard of him, or because of his own conceptual and technical limitations. The same could be said of the majority of Madrid painters who worked during the first third of the nineteenth century. Amongst them one might single out Andrés Rossi, an almost-unknown artist of Italian descent who was probably born in or around 1771, perhaps in Seville or Cadiz. He was a pupil at the San Fernando Academy, where he was a prize winner at the age of eighteen. He illustrated the treatise, *Exelencias del pincel y del buril*, by José Moreno de Texada, but his works tend more towards the evocation of a distant past – taking inspiration from Cerezo or Recco – than the present, and certainly do not anticipate the future.[162]

Given Goya's influence on the history of Spanish art, and his effect upon the life and work of many of the artists mentioned above, we must now turn to some of the important events that occurred at the end of the eighteenth century in order to place the Aragonese master in his due historical context. These determining factors affected the entire Hispanic world, on both sides of the Atlantic.

The End of the Eighteenth Century

The death of Charles III in 1788, preceding by only a few months the storming of the Bastille in Paris (14 July 1789), marked the beginning of a new period of conflict under his successor, Charles IV. Some problems had been left unsolved by the governments of Charles III – amongst others, corruption, nepotism, poverty, and disorganization – and the end-of-century crisis intensified. Around 1790 Spain fluctuated between two alternatives: innovation or tradition. A considerable sector of the clergy, and of the rural nobility from the provinces and the colonies, remained wedded to deeply rooted customs and privileges, which were comfortable but obsolete. Matters were made worse by the fact that the majority of Spaniards identified more with a messianic fanaticism than with the lessons, often pedantic, to be learned from Enlightenment thinkers.

The huge task which Charles III entrusted to those in power, although necessary to achieve his objectives for modernization, was greatly under funded, and events, as they unfolded, made the achievement of his goals all the more difficult. His efforts could have been crowned with success, even taking into account the indecisive nature of his successor, Charles IV, if the French Revolution had not brought about a change in internal Spanish politics. The all-powerful favourite, Minister Godoy, annulled part of the programme of reforms, keeping only the external apparatus of enlightened despotism: ministerial omnipresence and administrative dictatorship. For two decades the revolutionary spirit took root in people's minds and exploded in 1808 with the fall of the Bourbon dynasty. Some were attracted by the dynastic ideal and others by the enthusiastic and powerful dreams which arose with the French Revolution.

162 Ossorio y Bernard, 1883-1884; Cavestany, 1936-1940; Pérez Sánchez, 1983-1984; Pérez Sánchez, 1987.

The sequence of events is well known. In 1808, the Aranjuez rising obliged Charles IV to abdicate in favour of his son Ferdinand VII. Immediately after, Napoleon requested a meeting with the royal family and, whilst holding them captive, he convinced both to renounce the throne in favour of his own brother. He then invaded Spain. At the same time an uprising occurred which marked the beginning of the long and destructive War of Independence. Whilst this was ravaging the country, Napoleon installed Joseph I on the Spanish throne. After a brief reign of five years, in the midst of an enormously widespread conflict, he was forced to leave the country. At that time the famous Cortes of Cadiz drew up the first constitution (1812). Once the Napoleonic armies had been defeated, Ferdinand VII was reinstated as King (1814): he rejected these liberal constitutional reforms and both liberals and *afrancesados* (as supporters of the French during the Peninsular War were known) were equally repressed, whether they were patriots or supposed traitors. Growing agitation in the colonies resulted in a general uprising in Spain's territories in America. Between 1810 and 1825, a whole constellation of nations achieved their independence. Only Cuba, Puerto Rico, and the Philippines remained loyal to the Spanish crown until the so-called 'disaster' of 1898.

The history of Spain at the beginning of the nineteenth century was determined by a period of continuous crisis, with all kinds of confrontations and civil disputes which continued well into the century. Goya was witness to the horrific and complex, but doubtless interesting, events of this difficult period, which he faithfully recorded and

Fig. 59: Francisco de Goya,
Still Life with Bream
Oil on canvas, 44,8 x 62,5 cm
Houston (Texas), The Museum of Fine Arts

analysed in his extraordinary *oeuvre*. Francisco de Goya y Lucientes (1746-1828) (fig. 59), the most important figure in Spanish art of the eighteenth century and the period of transition into the nineteenth, is also one of the greatest names in the history of painting. His talent was limitless. He painted in numerous styles, worked with a variety of techniques, and actively experimented with different methods. As a painter, engraver, lithographer, draughtsman, and miniaturist, he has left an extensive body of work which ranges from portraits to genre painting, historical themes, horrific fantasies, mythology, moral allegories, and religious narratives, to name but a few of the fields in which he excelled. His evolution as a painter was slow, and he reached artistic maturity only in advanced years. In his last works, he laid the foundations of modern painting, since his canvases anticipate impressionism as well as, or perhaps more obviously, expressionism. He is even a subconscious precursor of surrealism. Goya's artistic formation began in the Rococo period, although neoclassical concepts had already begun to appear at that stage. The visual art scene during the reign of Charles III was brilliant, jovial, and disinterested in whatever did not concern the pure concept of art itself, revealing a joyful aristocratic and bourgeois self-confidence. Such a tendency is evident in flower and other still life pictures from the period, which convey a sense of optimism and an eminently refined beauty. Goya's work thus constitutes a rather abrupt and dramatic contrast with the official atmosphere. At the beginning of the nineteenth century, after successive personal crises, Goya began to work in a new direction, infiltrating the peaceable, calm world of the still life with a crude and direct simplicity. This radical shift had much to do with the disheartening upheavals which Spain was experiencing — she seemed to be on the brink of a bottomless abyss.

Goya's first still lifes appeared in templates for fabric, which were not greatly different from those of his colleagues at the Royal Workshop.[163] Essentially, they depicted hunting scenes with arms, dogs, cages with birds as bait, dead partridges and hares, and other objects. These were combined in tapestries with figures, surrounded by small details such as utensils or artistic tools, all of which were subordinate to the overall effect of the composition. It was not until the last years of his life, after 1800, that Goya truly dedicated himself to still lifes, executing them with the same sense of novelty and interpretative power that is characteristic of his works as a whole.

In the inventory of Goya's possessions, drawn up after his death by his wife, Josefa Bayeu, twelve still lifes are mentioned amongst the works bequeathed to his son, Javier. As a result of recent research, ten of them have been identified.[164] They are all painted with great sobriety and are characterised by broad brush-strokes and a rich palette. Dark blacks, golden browns, and daring touches of white, yellow, and red predominate. The motif of a dead animal, placed amongst everyday objects, prevails over the various elements of the compositions: plucked birds, birds of different species, hares, whole fish or cutlets, pieces of red meat, chops and fillets, as well as kitchen implements.[165]

Goya's still lifes convey a special energy and a surprising dynamism, as if they were melting pots overflowing with a violence bursting to escape. It is the feeling of death and sacrifice, the impression of a final heartbeat, the loss of life, which makes them so shocking. The Aragonese painter, used to contemplating, depicting, and weighing up the great number of visual impressions which bombarded him, never once let slip an artistic innovation. At some point he must have studied Meléndez's still lifes, whether in the Royal Collection or in the houses which he frequented. It may, indeed, be the case that he knew Meléndez, who died in 1780, since Madrid art circles were small enough to encourage such personal contact. Certain aspects of Meléndez's work are evident in Goya's still lifes, although they are transformed by his highly personal style. Goya had a moving and vital understanding of objects, and, in comparison to Meléndez, his works are much more static and solemn, since the painter from Fuendetodos had long given up the cult of precociousness in favour of expressionism. The rigorous structural

163 Sambricio, 1946; Madrid, 1995-1996; Madrid, 1996.

164 López Rey, 1948.

165 Pérez Sánchez, 1983-1984.

sense of his compositions and their chromatic richness reflect, however, the legacy of the past which was available to him, possibly in the palace in Aranjuez, where the forty still lifes painted by Meléndez for Charles IV, whilst he was Prince of Asturias, are displayed. Goya, like Meléndez, employed neutral backgrounds, but they were darker and full of foreboding. They gave his works a greater sense of tangible reality, and tended to create a threatening impression.

Goya necessarily adopted a different method of representing nature. Meléndez sometimes painted objects which he had before him, on other occasions he copied previous pictures of his own, and this direct approach gave to each of the details of his pictures a coherence and a scientific validity; he thus strived consciously for an authentic sense of verisimilitude. Goya, on the other hand, probably visualised the objects first, and then painted them, having elaborated a series of mental images through which he reinterpreted nature in his own particular way.

The use of light is also different in each painter. In Meléndez's compositions, it is distributed in a clear, transparent, uniform way, projected from a source beyond the left of the picture frame. It is used to reveal the textures of each of the objects illuminated, revealing them in the fullness of their volume and quality. But Goya, despite initially having used the same approach for the depiction of objects, became much more severe in his use of lighting effects, playing with contrasts of light and shade and a tenebrism which confers a sinister air upon his pictures. As a result, the spectator has before his eyes a world full of expressive intensity and obsessive anxiety which is sometimes cruel and which corresponds to a different reality, anticipating many of the aesthetic principles which would condition the evolution of this singular genre throughout the nineteenth century and give it a character very different from the spirit of Meléndez.[166]

Translator's note
A The word *bodegón* is the standard Spanish translation of still life, but it has been retained here on occasion as it carries an echo of its origins in *bodega*, denoting variously a tavern or bar, a cellar or winery, and a grocery store. The specificity of this resonance is absent from the English.

166 Faré, 1962; Bordeaux, 1978; Sterling, 1981.

Catalogue
Peter Cherry
& Juan J. Luna

1. Still Life with Small Pears, Bread, Earthenware Bowl and Glass Bottle

Oil on canvas: 47.8 x 34.6 cm
Signed on the table-top:
L^S. M^Z. D^{ZO}. AÑO 1760
Madrid: Prado Museum,
no. 912

Provenance
Royal Collections, Casita
del Príncipe, El Escorial;
Palacio Real de Aranjuez.

Bibliography
Soria, 1948, p. 216; Tufts,
1971, p. 168; Luna, 1982-
1983, p. 48, no. 2; Tufts,
1982, no. 11; Gutiérrez
Alonso, 1983, pp. 162-163;
Pérez Sánchez, 1983-1984,
p. 163, no. 146; Tufts, 1985a,
p. 62; Luna, 1995, p. 60;
Cherry and Luna, 2004, p.
156, no. 1; Garrido y Cherry,
2004 [in print], no. 912.

Exhibitions
Madrid-Barcelona, 1982-
1983, no. 2; Madrid,
1983-1984, no. 146; Raleigh-
Dallas-New York, 1985,
no. 3; Paris, 1987-1988,
no. 83; Madrid, 2004, no. 1.

On top of a rough-hewn wooden table, displayed with such details as the grooves and knots which form part of the wood, some small pears (known as St John's pears) are spread around the foreground space in no particular order; a loaf of bread appears in the middle distance and beside it rises a tall tapered jug, very white and covered in a glaze which contains a component of tin. The jug, of the type popularly known in Spain as "a jug with four spouts", could well be from Andalusia – from Andújar or Triana. A system of stylised decorations, embossed in a series of linear ridges resembling roof tiles, covers the exterior of the jug, whose two handles are finely moulded in an undulating shape; the four spouts are expertly tapered. Ceramic vessels of this kind also appear in certain canvases by Zurbarán and Murillo from the previous century; this is a testament to the slow artistic evolution of such decorated ware. Ornate jugs like the one in the picture were fashioned and are still produced as part of a long-standing tradition in such towns as Agost (Alicante), La Rambla and Lucena (Córdoba), and Vera (Almería). In the background of this still life, an earthenware bowl, covered over by a metal lid and displaying a protruding spoon, is discernible; alongside, a glass bottle containing wine completes the composition.

There are some special qualities about the picture which need to be explained. Firstly, it was signed and dated in the year 1760; this indicates that, according to our present knowledge, it is one of the earliest still lifes painted in Spain by Meléndez. Its formula of composition, the arrangement and depiction of the objects, and the dimensions of the canvas itself suggest comparisons with other works by the same artist in the Prado Museum (cats 2, 6); it is likely that those works were also painted around the same time. The three canvases, therefore, belong to the first group of still lifes executed by Meléndez while he was employed at the Royal Palace in Madrid.

Other curious details in the picture are the *pentimenti* clearly visible among the dark shadows which surround some of the surface details over the loaf of bread and to the left of the jug. It is obvious that the executed picture was preceded by a long period of painstaking preparation; it is also worth noting that this work displays certain incipient characteristics which were later developed in his mature *oeuvre*. **J.J.L.**

7. 591.

2. Still Life with a Plate of Cherries, Plums, Cheese and a Jug

Oil on Canvas: 47 x 34 cms.
Signed on the underside
of the jug: L.S. M.Z.
Madrid.Prado Museum,
no. 911

Provenance
Royal Collections, Casita
del Príncipe, El Escorial;
Palacio Real de Aranjuez.

Bibliography
Espasa Calpe XXXIV, p. 640;
M. Soria, 1948, p. 216; F.J.
Sánchez Cantón, 1965, fig.
206; E. Tufts, 1971, p. 168; R.
Torres Martín, 1971, fig. 17;
J.J. Luna, 1982-1983, p. 52,
no. 4; E. Tufts, 1982, no. 10;
L.C. Gutiérrez Alonso, 1983,
pp. 163-164; E. Tufts, 1985,
pp. 62-63; J.J. Luna, 1995,
p. 62; C. Garrido and
P. Cherry, 2004 (in print),
no. 911.

Exhibitions
Madrid-Barcelona, 1982-
1983, no. 4; Valencia, 1984,
no. 3; Raleigh-Dallas-
New York, 1985, no. 4.

The object which immediately attracts the attention of the spectator is the spectacular earthenware jug with its white enameled surface and its twisted handle, which is reminiscent of a Solomonic pillar; the glaze on the jug is achieved by the use of tin oxide: this was common practice in the eighteenth century. Beside the jug, a section of cheese forms a contrast with the play of straight and crooked lines which demarcate it, in the same way as the very distinct planes of light which the cheese reflects; directly in front, a dish, decorated in the Rococo style and with a wavy pattern at its edges, is displayed full to the brim with cherries. A few plums are positioned in the lower right-hand corner of the picture.

When one analyses the jug, which is painted in a cobalt blue, it is immediately evident that it forms part of the ware specifi-cally crafted in Talavera (although such jugs were also produced in Puente de Arzobispo and in Toledo) where it received the colloquial name of *jarra de bola* (jug in the shape of a bowl) or *jarra de borracho* (a wine drinker's jug), because its primary function was as a container of wine. This type of crockery has been classified, because of its specific floral decoration, as belonging to the class known as *la adormidera* (the opium poppy). However, Gutiérrez Alonso believes that the flower on this jug resembles a sunflower or a chrysant-hemum or something similar; for this reason, it is better to use the terms in common use when referring to decorated ware from

Talavera or Puente del Arzobispo, such as *de la rosilla* (a roseate pattern), *del ramito* (an entwining branch), or *de la letra* (a stylised letter pattern). The dish is probably also of Talaveran manufacture – of the decorated type known as *castañuela* (castanet). The above-mentioned characteristics also find an echo in other paintings by Meléndez, including no. 924 in the Prado Museum (cat. 22).

Other paintings in this artist's *oeuvre* display very similar characteristics, including the use of identical dishes and jugs – the jug shown here is used again in no.924 (cat. 22) – but without the floral decoration which distinguishes this canvas. However, such embellishment also features in the painting by Meléndez (also included in this exhibition) at the Museo Nacional d'Art de Catalunya; a copy of that work is to be found in the North Carolina Museum of Art.

Arguing from a purely technical point of view, this still life should be included among those painted by Meléndez in the 1760s. This theory is confirmed by the expressive force and impact of the shapes and volumes, as well as the visionary directness of the objects and the combined motifs of the fruits and utensils. In addition to this, light and colour combine to produce magnificent effects; one need only emphasise the wonderful impact of the bright reddish hues at the centre of the composition: these are set against yellow and white tones, both of which also display a bluish overlay. **J.J.L.**

7. 561.

3. Still Life with Figs, Bread and Wine

Oil on canvas, 47.6 x 34 cm.
Washington, National
Gallery of Art
Patron's Permanent Fund
no. 2000.6.1

Provenance
Mlle. Anna Petit, c.1895,
thence by descent; Private
collection, France; Edward
Speelman; Derek Johns Ltd.,
London (from whom
acquired by the present
owner).

Bibliography
Washington, National
Gallery of Art, 2000-2001,
pp. 44-45; Cherry and Luna,
2004, p. 158, no. 2.

Exhibitions
Madrid, 2004, no. 2

The combination of objects in this still life evokes a summer dessert. The main motif of a plate of figs is presented in the foreground, accompanied by a knife with which to eat the fruit and a loaf of bread. Behind these, there is an olive barrel, wine bottle and a wine cooler, whose lid has been removed to show the ice filling the cork receptacle that contains the wine-filled copper vessel.

This painting is a consummate example of Meléndez's careful orchestration of objects in still lifes of a demanding vertical format. The foreshortened knife acts as an important spatial indicator, that illusionistically projects over the table edge and points into the fictive depth of the picture. As with other pictures of this format in the exhibition, the dense composition encourages the viewer to read back into pictorial space in a zig-zag pattern from one overlapping and counterbalancing element to another, contemplating at every step Meléndez's abilities in accurately representing the familiar form, texture and colour of each. In this painting, as in *Still Life with Small Pears, Bread, Earthenware Bowl and Glass Bottle* (cat. 1), the crusty loaf of bread is a vehicle for Meléndez's extraordinary representational ability and, unsurprisingly, became a *leitmotif* of his still lifes.

The plate of fruit originally contained wild strawberries or, perhaps, mulberries, and a wedge of cheese in the right foreground. The original fruits may have been painted out for chromatic reasons and, even to the naked eye, these are visible through the worn lake pigment of the purple figs as small points of red colour. Adjustments to the right-hand contour of the bottle and its highlights, and the contours of the bread can also be seen. Below the grey background tone, the ghostly outline of the lid of the wine cooler tilted at an angle can be made out, that is similar to this motif in *Still Life with Lemons, Oranges, Azaroles and Watermelon* (fig. 60). Such drastic repainting was not uncommon in Meléndez's still lifes and is a measure of his uncompromising desire to achieve an optimum result in his paintings. **P.C.**

Fig. 60: Luis Meléndez, *Still Life with Lemons, Oranges, Azaroles and Watermelon*
Oil on canvas, 47.8 x 34.3 cm
Madrid, Prado Museum, no. 913

4. Still Life with Plums, Pears and Basket of Fruit

Oil on canvas, 48 x 35 cm.
Masaveu collection

Provenance
Georg Schäffer,
Schweinfurt; Harari and
Johns Ltd., London (from
whom acquired by the
present owner).

Bibliography
Cherry and Luna, 2004,
p. 160, no. 3.

Exhibitions
Madrid, 2004, no. 3.

This still life depicts an appetising display of summer fruits, with pears, plums and grapes, and the detail of fruit on the branch, as in other pictures by Meléndez, conveys the impression that this has been recently picked. The central motif of a small basket full of fruit also appears in a number of other pictures by the artist, such as *Still Life with Peaches, Plums and Honey Pot* (cat. 5).

The painting also exemplifies the compositional harmony Meléndez habitually sought in paintings of a vertical format, through arrangements of counterbalancing interrelated forms that occupy different planes of pictorial space and recede broadly in accordance with the principles of perspective. As was usual in his still lifes, Meléndez sought maximum pictorial effect from the placement of the objects. The basket is turned so that its handle is set at an oblique angle to the table edge and points into the picture space, as do the sharply foreshortened wooden spoon and jug handle. Indeed, the spoon and basket handle can be read together almost as perspectival orthogonals that articulate pictorial depth. Meléndez demarcates the different planes of the painting, by placing one form in front of another on the table top, whose depth is marked by the plum branch that probes the space at the back of the basket and the single plum overlapping the front edge of the table. The terracotta jug that closes off the composition in the background has been painted around the basket of fruit and bowls, and Meléndez's use of soft brushes and broader detail in this motif implies the effect of atmospheric perspective. Examination by x-radiograph shows that Meléndez originally painted the plate of plums with a scalloped edge, of a type that he used in *Still Life with Figs, Bread and Wine* (cat. 3). Its definitive straight edge was possibly chosen in order to rhyme the plate with the bowls in the middle ground. Although this change seems a comparatively minor one, it reveals Meléndez's concern with the aesthetic quality of every detail of his works. **P.C.**

5. Still Life with Peaches, Plums and Honey Pot

Oil on canvas, 48.5 x 33.5 cm.
Signed: L.ᶳ M.ᶻ
Plácido Arango collection

Provenance
Frederick Mont collection,
New York; Newhouse
Galleries, New York; Georg
Schäfer, Schweinfurt; Pascal
Sernet Sale, Paris, 2 June,
1986 (when acquired by the
present owner).

Bibliography
Tufts, 1985, no. 89; Cherry
and Luna, 2004, p. 162, no. 4.

Exhibitions
Madrid, 2004, no. 4.

The soft brushes that Meléndez used to model the luminous golden peaches in the foreground of this painting help to convey a sense of the downy texture of the fruit skins and the impression of three dimensionality in their indistinct contours. The Manises-ware honey pot shown in the centre of the painting was a favourite type of object painted by Meléndez throughout his career. This can be seen in two other paintings of a vertical format in the exhibition (cats 6, 7), in which it occupies a similar place in the middle ground, just to the right of centre, with fruits arranged around it. While the pot is an important compositional feature – a vertical accent that marks the middle ground - Meléndez evidently also relished representing the play of light on its glazed surface. A change to its left-hand side can be seen with the naked eye, that made its proportions broader and ensured a more aesthetically satisfying relationship with the other elements in the painting. Meléndez frequently made such adjustments to the shapes and proportions of objects in his still lifes for reasons of pictorial necessity.

Meléndez planned the composition of this still life in terms of the relationships between the primary forms – peaches, honey pot and basket of plums – and added the boldly painted branches of plums in subsequent painting sessions. The honey pot and peaches are seen behind a screen of plums on the branch, that were literally superimposed over these finished motifs. The handle of the basket may have been a late addition to the picture and appears to have been painted over the green plums. By occupying different points in pictorial depth, the plum branches at once mark and connect the different planes of the picture. These secondary elements are also played off against the large forms to enrich and vary the composition. Meléndez often resolved compositions with strateg--ically placed loose fruits at the front of the table edge that were painted late in the development of the painting, as can be seen here in the purple plums and by the fact that the single green plum is painted over the contour of the right-hand peach. **P.C.**

6. Still Life with Oranges, Honey Pot, Box of Sweetmeats and Watermelons

Oil on canvas: 48.3 x 34.5 cm
Signed on top of one of
the cartons: L.M.
Madrid: Prado Museum,
no. 910

Provenance
Royal Collections, Casita
del Príncipe, El Escorial;
Palacio Real de Aranjuez.

Bibliography
Aguilera, 1946, lám. xiii;
Soria, 1948, p. 216; Gaya
Nuño, 1950, p. 150; Lastic,
1955, p. 40; Lastic, 1955, no.
9, p. 20; Tufts, 1971, p. 167;
Luna, 1982-1983, p. 50,
no. 3; Tufts, 1982, no. 9;
Gutiérrez Alonso, 1983,
p. 163; Tufts, 1985a, p. 63;
Luna, 1995, p. 64; Cherry
and Luna, 2004, p. 164, no. 5;
Garrido y Cherry, 2004
[in print], no. 910.

Exhibitions
Madrid-Barcelona, 1982-
1983, no. 3; Valencia, 1984,
no. 4; Raleigh-Dallas-New
York, 1985, no. 5; Madrid,
1990-1991, no. 67; Bilbao,
1999-2000, no. 43; Madrid,
2004, no. 5.

The interest of the artist in assessing the pure geometric forms which underlie natural objects, is given free rein here; he establishes a compromise between a veristic representation of the surrounding reality and his obvious desire to depict forms and shapes in as refined a way as possible. Thus, the objects included here are presented almost as little spheres, parallelepipeds, a cylinder, and two large spheres; in fact, they are oranges, boxes of sweets, melons and a pot of honey (from Manises, near Valencia) whose glazed surface contains a component of tin. This studied sensation of pure shapes and forms is intensified by the complete absence of extraneous details and minute objects, which would only distract the spectator's attention from the awesome contemplation of the strong luminous effects applied with consummate exactitude, and of the assured coordination of contrasted colours and tonalities.

The objects depicted are similar to those which appear in other still lifes by the artist; the ease with which they are reproduced over and over again is a good indication that Meléndez made use of them in his domestic environment. The finesse with which the pot of honey is rendered is truly outstanding, both in its essence and in its contrast with the tonalities of the surroundings: the pot's whitish hues are set against the greens, oranges and ochres which predominate in the other pictorial elements. **J.J.L.**

7. *Still Life with Oranges, Honey Pots and Boxes of Sweets*

Oil on canvas, 48 x 36 cm.
Signed on end of box
of sweets: M.ᶻ
Fort Worth, Texas, Kimbell
Art Museum

Provenance
Private collection,
Switzerland; Harari and
Johns Ltd., London; Kimbell
Museum, Fort Worth,
Texas (acquired 1985).

Bibliography
Pillsbury, Cummings,
Jordan, 1987, pp. 260-261;
Luna, 1989, pp. 372-373;
Cherry and Luna, 2004,
p. 166, no. 6.

Exhibitions
Madrid, 2004, no. 6.

This painting and *Still Life with Oranges, Honey Pot, Boxes of Sweetmeats and Watermelons* from the royal collection (cat. 6) demonstrate Meléndez's ability to paint original variations on similar still life themes. The artist's acumen for seeing ever new formal and compositional possibilities in the same elements is partly due to his grasp of the underlying geometric character of objects. On an almost "abstract" level, then, in both pictures intense visual satisfaction derives from the geometric interplay between the spherical fruit, rectangular boxes and tubular pot, that is only emphasised by the insistent illusion of three-dimensionality of the forms.

Meléndez is also scrupulous in describing the particular surface characteristics of each of the objects in the composition. The care with which he has painted differently textured objects is evident here, describing in detail the light effects on the glazed surface of the pot, orange peel and splintered sheets of rough wood of the sweetmeat boxes. Some wrinkling of the paint on the end of the box that bears Meléndez's signature, as if scorched into the wood, suggests that he repainted this area at a late stage, most probably to ensure that its tonality was consistent with the illusionistic perspectival projection of the box at this point. There is nothing schematic in Meléndez's modulation of colour and gradation of tone that creates the illusion of volume in the oranges. Reflected light illuminates the shaded parts of the fruit and patches of green describe unevenly ripened skin, while pointillist touches of yellow, pink and white paint laid over the orange body colour of the fruit evoke the lightfall on its pitted surface. All of this testifies to Meléndez's consummate ability to translate into painted form his close scrutiny of the objects before him. **P.C.**

8. *Still Life with Melon, Jug and Bread*

Oil on canvas, 47 x 35.5 cm.
Signed: L. M.^Z
Valladolid, Museo Nacional
de Escultura

Provenance
Prince of Asturias; Casita
del Príncipe, El Escorial;
Palacio Real, Aranjuez;
Valladolid, Museo Nacional
de Escultura.

Bibliography
Tufts, 1985, no. 16; Luna,
1995, no. 12; Cherry and
Luna, 2004, p. 170, no. 8.

Exhibitions
Valladolid, Museo Nacional
de Escultura, 2001, no.53;
Madrid, 2004, no. 8.

This is one of Meléndez's most dense compositions, in which intensely plastic natural and man-made objects are compacted into a narrow vertical field, to the almost complete exclusion of ambient space. A cantaloupe melon occupies the foreground; this seems to be pushed forward by a jug capped with a bowl and a small corked bottle in the middle ground; while in the background there is a basket with bread, a knife, a wooden spoon, three plates and a kitchen cloth. The description of contrasting textures in the painting is particularly impressive, as is the close observation of lightfall on different surfaces; the highlights on glass, metal, ceramic glazes and grape skins, and the absorbtion of light by other materials.

The melon is the real protagonist of this still life and is daringly placed in the foreground, so that its large spherical mass all but eclipses the other objects. Meléndez's modulation of earth tones in painting this fruit creates a powerful illusion of its volume and his use of glazes of black pigment give the impression of its segments and the characteristic depressions in its surface. Meléndez has also depicted with extraordinary accuracy the reticulated skin of this type of melon, using intricate brushwork to describe the light and shade of each of the individual ridges of its complex surface. The melon can be considered a *tour de force* of Meléndez's ability to imitate nature and it is not surprising that he reprised this challenging motif in a number of his most accomplished still lifes (fig. 61). **P.C.**

Fig. 61: Luis Meléndez, *Still Life with Melon, Pears and a Basket of Bread*, h.1770
Oil on canvas, 61,9 x 85,1 cm
Boston, Museum of Fine Arts

9. *Still Life with Bread, Bottle and Jug*

Oil on canvas, 48 x 34.5 cm.
Principado de Asturias,
Masaveu collection
(on extended loan to Oviedo,
Museo de Bellas Artes de
Asturias)

Bibliography
Tufts, 1985, no. 91; Luna,
1995, no. 20; Cherry and
Luna, 2004, p. 172, no. 9.

Exhibitions
Oviedo 1995, no. 21; Seville –
Madrid – Oviedo, 1996-
1997, no. 29; Madrid, 2004,
no. 9.

This painting depicts two large, round loaves of fine white bread and a knife, a wine bottle and an Alcorcón jug with a wooden spoon in it, capped by a broken plate. Meléndez's choice of rounded objects of different shapes and volumes and their strategic placement in this composition has resulted in one of his most impressive still life paintings. The formal presence of the objects is enhanced by the light background of a neutral earth tone and the studied modulation of light and shade in the picture. Both loaves on the tabletop are drawn in sharp foreshortening, although the left-hand one has been tilted at an angle to create a more compelling perspective effect, in a manner similar to the lid of the box of jelly in *Still Life with Limes, Box of Jelly, Butterfly and Kitchen Utensils.* (cat. 24). The emphatic foreshortening of this loaf is underscored by the knife beneath it, that is angled to point into depth and metaphorically cuts through pictorial space. Meléndez has composed the picture so that the angle of the tilted bread is echoed in that of the wooden spoon and is even, it seems, picked up in the random tracks of glaze of the jug. Without wishing to over simplify the subtle formal relations between the objects in this picture, the composition is bound together on the basis of two interlocking diagonal axes; the loaves of bread and knife guide the gaze towards the wine bottle, while the angled profile of the left-hand bread points in the counterbalancing direction of the wooden spoon.

Relatively spare compositions such as this one have the effect of focusing attention on Meléndez's consummate descriptive powers in his representation of the different textures of the objects, bread, glass and ceramic. The uppermost loaf has been tilted up into the light to allow the artist to describe the smooth, undulating surface of its crust and distinctive circular decoration. In the bread, a detailed account is also given of the seams joining the upper and lower crusts, with close attention paid to the cracks caused in the baking and a break in the lower bread revealing its soft interior. In this particularly carefully painted still life, Meléndez achieves a consummate illusion of reality. This desire may also have caused a change in his technique; the particularly smooth surface of this painting, and its companion (cat. 10), may be due Meléndez's use of a preparatory layer to even out his habitual open weave canvas canvas and provide a finer surface on which to work. **P.C.**

10. *Still Life with Grapes and Melon, Bread Roll, Cheese, Jug and Glass*

Oil on canvas, 48 x 34.5
Signed on table edge
at right: L. M^Z.
Principado de Asturias,
Masaveu collection
(on extended loan to Oviedo,
Museo de Bellas Artes de
Asturias)

Bibliography
Tufts, 1985, no. 92; Luna,
1995, no. 21; Cherry and
Luna, 2004, p. 174, no. 10.

Exhibitions
Oviedo 1995, no. 22; Seville -
Madrid - Oviedo, 1996-1997,
no. 30; Madrid, 2004, p. 174,
no. 10.

This still life represents a complete dessert of fruit — a single apple, black grapes and a watermelon — with bread and cheese and a jug with a drinking glass placed in its mouth. In this case, the jug probably contained water, since the glass with a square handle is of a common contemporary type used to drink water, made at the Real Fábrica de la Granja and elsewhere. In this composition, the objects are composed to maximise the fictive depth of the picture; the apple fulfills an illusionistic function in slightly overlapping the table edge, with the bread, cheese and grapes arranged on a diagonal receding into the left-hand background, and the watermelon and jug behind them placed along an analagous line. The smaller objects are placed in front of large, swelling forms of the watermelon and jug; watermelons serve to close off the background in a similar way in *Still Life with Oranges, Honey Pot, Boxes of Sweetmeats and Watermelons* (cat. 6). The composition is, however, also constructed on two intersecting diagonal accents; the eye connects a sequence of asymmetrically balanced forms in one direction from the bread in the foreground to the jug in the background, and in another from the apple to the watermelon. The bread roll is clearly closely related to the same motif in a similar position in *Still Life with a Dish of Plums,*

Figs and Bread Roll (cat. 17), although it is not possible to tell from sheer observation which of these was painted first.

The objects have been chosen and juxtaposed for both formal and textural contrast. The light effects on the smooth skins of different fruits are carefully observed, while the bread crust, cheese and glass are objects with a greater degree of textural incident. Perhaps the most admirable motif is the glass in the mouth of the earthenware jug. Glassware has always been regarded as one of the most challenging motifs for the still life painter and here it becomes a vehicle for a supreme demonstration of Meléndez's representational ability, in describing the greenish hue of the transparent glass and the complex play of light on its surface. The effect of transparency in the glass is achieved in a logical manner by glazing paint over the already completed lip of the jug, although this approach did not allow Meléndez to register the inevitable distortion to the lip of the jug seen through the curved wall of the glass. Meléndez's indifference to this optical phenomenon raises the possibility that the glass was an afterthought in the development of the painting. A pentimento at the lower point of the rim of the glass observable with the naked eye shows that the motif was not achieved without effort. **P.C.**

11. Still Life with Ham, Eggs, Bread and Kitchen Utensils

Oil on Canvas: 49 x 37 cms.
Madrid. Prado Museum,
no. 934

Provenance
Royal Collections, Casita
del Príncipe, El Escorial;
Palacio Real de Aranjuez.

Bibliography
M. Soria, 1948, p. 217;
P. Guinard y J. Baticle, 1950,
p. 138; G. de Lastic, 1955,
p. 42; Id. 1955, no. 9, p. 22;
F.J. Sánchez Cantón, 1965,
fig. 207; E. Tufts, 1971, p. 175;
J.J. Luna, 1982-1983, p. 66,
no. 11; E. Tufts, 1982, no. 33;
L.C. Gutiérrez Alonso, 1983,
p. 164; E. Tufts, 1985, p. 65;
J.J. Luna, 1995, p. 72; C.
Garrido and P. Cherry, 2004
(in print), no. 934.

Exhibitions
London, 1954-1955, no. 13;
London, 1963-1964, no. 18;
Madrid-Barcelona, 1982-
1983, no. 11; Valencia, 1984,
no. 10; Paris, 1987-1988,
no. 85; Geneva 1989, no. 53;
Frankfurt, 1999-2002,
no. 106.

A large ceramic cooking-pot of Alcorcón manufacture (of a type which features in other works by Meléndez) dominates the canvas here; the pot is covered over by a fragment of a tile, over which a large wooden spoon is partially visible. One could almost say with total conviction that this solid ceramic vessel is the main object of interest in the picture, because its bulk is rendered in a fittingly consistent way; this unadorned and monumental vessel makes an impressive statement in the expressive quality of its convex shape. In front of it, a large piece of ham and two eggs fill up the foreground, along with a small, shiny metal frying-pan, whose large handle is raised diagonally towards the background, terminating at the rear of the cooking pot. An earthenware bowl, along with a metal lid and a loaf of bread, fills the space in the background. Thus connections are established between the picture's motifs and the dark neutral colours which mark the compositions' most distant point, against which the objects are silhouetted with an impressive economy and clarity of line.

One of the greatest achievements of the artist's technical skill here is the ease with which the forms are rendered; in each case, the volumes of the structures are fittingly reproduced with a surprisingly vigorous quality: outlines, colours and, above all, the impact of light play their part in bestowing on the picture a character of forthrightness and expressiveness. These aspects are immediately obvious to the viewer. The colour textures in the paintings are also subtly differentiated: such details are immediately made manifest when the elements on the canvas are examined and compared in all their diversity.

A copy of this picture is included in a private collection in Madrid; however, its mediocre workmanship makes it likely to be a product of the nineteenth century. This is known to have happened with other still lifes by Meléndez. J.J.L.

587.

12. Still Life with Herrings, Spring Onions, Bread and Kitchen Utensils

Oil on canvas: 50.3 x 36.7 cm
Madrid: Prado Museum,
no. 907

Provenance
Royal Collections, Casita
del Príncipe, El Escorial;
Palacio Real de Aranjuez.

Bibliography
Aguilera, 1946, lám. x;
Enciclopedia, n.d., p. 640;
Soria, 1948, p. 216; Tufts,
1971, p. 166; Luna, 1982-
1983, p. 60, no. 8; Tufts,
1982, no. 6; Gutiérrez
Alonso, 1983, p. 164; Tufts,
1985a, pp. 63 and 65; Luna,
1995, p. 70; Cherry and
Luna, 2004, p. 178, no. 12;
Garrido and Cherry, 2004
[in print], no. 907.

Exhibitions
Bordeaux-Paris-Madrid,
1979-1980, no. 40 (Span.
ed.); Madrid-Barcelona,
1982-1983, no. 8; Valencia,
1984, no. 7; Madrid, 1988-
1989, no. 69; Madrid, 2004,
no. 12.

In the foreground, some smoked herrings (kippers), with their rugged contours, form a contrast with the polished smoothness of a bunch of spring onions nearby; alongside, a loaf of bread – shaped like a dome – combines notes of clarity and solidity. In the middle distance, a broad-bellied ceramic vessel, which could be either a pitcher or a cooking pot, hits the eye; the vessel is almost completely covered by a decorated piece of broken tile whose design indicates that the provenance is Talavera de la Reina (Toledo) or Puente del Arzobispo: the decoration on the tile (which partly obscures the Alcorcón bowl directly behind) is of the type known as *rosilla* (i.e. with a pattern of roses) or *ramito* (so called because of the delicate interlace of branches and tendrils). The large wooden handle of a spoon is wedged between the fragment of tile and the rim of the pitcher. An olive-oil funnel, an earthenware vessel used for vinegar, and a basket complete the composition, confirming the artist's desire to convey an authentic impression of *verisimilitude* in his canvas.

The composition is worked out with a key emphasis on verticality and, unlike many other works by Meléndez, the rather cluttered accumulation of the depicted objects evinces a certain *horror vacui*; this element makes the picture stand out from other examples of the artist's production from the same period. Indeed, when one contemplates the individual motifs, it is obvious that this work is infused with an air of originality, because some of the elements do not appear elsewhere in his canvases. It is most likely that the work was executed at some time between 1760 and 1770; a certain palpable lack of refinement in the design suggests that the date of completion should be assigned to the early 1760s. J.J.L.

13. Still Life with Cauliflower and Basket of Fish, Eggs and Leeks

Oil on canvas, 49.5 x 36.5 cm.
Private collection

Provenance
Georg Schäffer,
Schweinfurt; Jan Dik
collection, Switzerland;
Private collection, Canada.

Bibliography
Tufts, 1985, no. 66; Cherry
and Luna, 2004, p. 176,
no. 11.

Exhibitions
Raleigh-Dallas-New York,
1985, no. 8; Madrid, 2004,
p. 176, no. 11.

The main protagonist of this picture is the cauliflower in the right foreground, that is accompanied by garlic and spices, and a shopping basket filled with market produce; fish, eggs, leeks and a brown paper cone of legumes. These objects are bathed in a silvery light and set against a background of a neutral tone that lightens towards the right-hand side of the painting. Many of the objects in Meléndez's paintings appear familiar and well-used, and the basket is no exception, having been repaired with string at its left side. Although an apparently insignificant detail, this constitutes a "proof" that Meléndez painted the motif from a real object in this condition, rather than from his memory or imagination. The tin funnel was evidently also a real object owned by the artist and appears with a basket, bowl and leeks in another kitchen still life of vertical format, *Still Life with Herings, Spring Onions, Bread and Kitchen Utensils* (cat. 12).

The composition of this picture is conceived in similar terms to *Still Life with Melon, Jug and Bread* (cat. 8), relying as it does on a large natural form in the right foreground, vessels in the left middle ground and a basket filled with objects in the background. This comparison shows how Meléndez was able to make the most of given compositional formulae by varying the objects in the arrangements and depicting these with such a high degree of

verismilitude. The close juxtaposition of man-made objects of different metals, ceramic and wicker work is, for instance, a studied demonstration of Meléndez's ability to describe the particular material qualities of each.

The painting was evidently well known enough in the eighteenth century to inspire a number of painted responses. One of these, *Still Life with Cauliflower and Kitchen Utensils* in the Museo Cerralbo (fig. 62), is a variant by an anonymous imitator who incorporated the cauliflower and copper pan into a horizontal composition of his own. However, it is a testament to Meléndez's skill that the imitator was unable to match his compositional subtlety and observation of structure and detail in the depiction of the cauliflower, whose nebulous florets appear more like cotton wool beside the original. **P.C.**

Fig. 62: Anonymous, *Still Life with Cauliflower and Kitchen Utensils*
Oil on canvas, 37 x 50 cm
Madrid, Museo Cerralbo

14. Still Life with Tomatoes, Aubergines and Onions

Oil on canvas, 36.8 x 49 cm.
Private collection; Courtesy
of Derek Johns Ltd., London

Provenance
Private collection, Spain;
Derek Johns Ltd., London.

Bibliography
Cherry and Luna, 2004,
p. 180, no. 13.

Exhibitions
Madrid, 2004, no. 13.

In this painting of deceptive simplicity, five tomatoes are arranged before a bowl of unripened aubergines and white onions. Meléndez concentrated his artistic attention on accurately representing the forms and surfaces of the whole vegetables. He modelled the tomatoes with a range of red hues and carefully applied highlights, and described the colour of the aubergine skins with bold touches of blue-green and yellow pigment, with a blush of the characteristic wine colour beginning to deepen in the ripening fruit. Although tomatoes had assumed their fundamental role in Spanish cuisine long before Meléndez's time, he was the first Spanish still life painter to give them due prominence in his paintings. They appear, for instance, in another *Still Life with Bread, Ham, Cheese and Vegetables* (fig. 63) and in an open-air context in *Still Life with Artichokes and Tomatoes in a Landscape* (fig. 64). Juan van der Hamen (1596-1631) was one of the few earlier Spanish still life painters to have included tomatoes in his paintings, such as *Still Life with Fruit Bowl and Sweets* (Madrid, Banco de España).

The painting demonstrates the effectiveness of Meléndez's habitual compositional strategies in transforming such unprepossessing and commonplace subject matter into a powerful aesthetic experience. Viewers share with the artist his fascination with the eccentric lobed "architecture" of the tomatoes. These are shown in the foreground of the painting and from a low viewpoint, that endows them with a monumentality that belies their "life-size" representation in the picture. The smallest tomato on the left-hand side creates a pseudo-perspectival effect that implies a greater depth to the picture than would exist in reality. Moreover, Meléndez has distilled a natural drama from the vital life forces that animate the flailing onion roots, writhing aubergine stalks and the fruit emerging from its casings. **P.C.**

Fig. 63: Luis Meléndez,
*Still Life with Bread, Ham,
Cheese and Vegetables*, h.1770
Oil on canvas, 63,8 x 85,1 cm
Boston, Museum of Fine Arts

Fig. 64: Luis Meléndez,
*Still Life with Artichokes and
Tomatoes in a Landscape*
Oil on canvas, 61,6 x 81,9 cm
Private collection

15. *Still Life with Cucumbers, Tomatoes and Kitchen Utensils*

Oil on canvas: 41.6 x 62.5 cm
Signed on the edge of the table: L.ˢ. Eᵒ. Mᶻ. D. Rᵃ Dᶻᵒ. ISᵗᵒ. Pᵉ. 1774
Madrid: Prado Museum, no. 930

Provenance

Royal Collections, Casita del Príncipe, El Escorial; Palacio Real de Aranjuez.

Bibliography

Onieva, 1956, lám. 22; Tufts, 1971, p. 174; Luna, 1982-1983, p. 134, no. 45; Tufts, 1982, no. 29; Gutiérrez Alonso, 1983, p. 166; Tufts, 1985a, pp. 85-86; Luna, 1995, p. 178; Cherry and Luna, 2004, p. 184, no. 15; Garrido and Cherry, 2004 [in print], no. 930.

Exhibitions

Madrid, 1950; Mexico, 1978, no. 60; Berlin, 1982, no. 4-13; Madrid-Barcelona, 1982-1983, no. 45; Valencia, 1984, no. 36; Raleigh-Dallas-New York, 1985, no. 34; Madrid, 1989-1990, no. 43; Madrid, 2004, no. 15.

This picture is unusual within the artist's *oeuvre* in that the abbreviated version of all his names is here included, along with the year of the work's execution. Here, the artist has combined the most characteristic ingredients of a simple salad, while at the same time exploiting the opportunity of including, beside the diverse tonalities of the cucumbers and tomatoes, an earthenware bowl of Alcorcón (Madrid) manufacture. This last item is partly covered by a plate which doubtless forms part of the stacked series of plates on the other side of the picture: these plates were obviously fashioned in Puente del Arzobispo. In addition, there is a bottle of vinegar, an olive-oil funnel and a salt cellar. These objects have functions which are obviously related, being designed for use at table, and as containers of condiments intended to enhance the flavour of the salad ingredients.

The association of the garden vegetables in the picture with the kitchen utensils allows the artist to establish qualitative comparisons between the distinct contours and surface details of all the motifs documented on the canvas; the artist's brush conveys the diverse textures of the assembled objects with consummate finesse. The composition, in which the objects appear to be placed at random, is arranged on top of a wooden plank, which serves as a makeshift table; the objects stand out, in part because of the dark, neutral background. A habitual characteristic of this artist's paintings – the emphasis with which the volumes and dimensions of the objects are delineated and differentiated – imparts a quality of relief sculpture to the work. The inclusion of the cucumbers is a peculiar feature, and their positioning and profusion make them the principal focus of interest in the work: the wrinkled texture of their rinds stands out in comparison with the smooth skins of the tomatoes and the brilliant sheen of the utensils, whose shapes are rendered with a rigorous attention to form. In aesthetic terms, the overall impression approximates to a geometric concept of unquestionable purity of design. J.J.L.

16. *Still Life with a Plate of White and Black Grapes*

Oil on Canvas 42 x 62 cms.
Signed: Egidius Ludovicus
Meléndez de Rivera Durazo
y Santo Padre, año de 1771.
Madrid. Prado Museum,
no. 904

Provenance
Royal Collections, Casita
del Príncipe, El Escorial;
Palacio Real de Aranjuez.

Bibliography
M. Soria, 1948, p. 216; E.
Tufts, 1971, p. 165; J.J. Luna,
1982-1983, p. 104, no. 30;
E. Tufts, 1982, no. 3; E. Tufts,
1985, p. 79; J.J. Luna, 1995,
p. 146; C. Garrido and P.
Cherry, 2004 (in print),
no. 904.

Exhibitions
Madrid-Barcelona, 1982-
1983, no. 30; Valencia, 1984,
no. 24.

A heaped – up pile of bunches of grapes, the whole effect resembling an architectural marvel, dominates the entire composition; the white and black grapes, covered over with vine leaves, are arranged in an apparently random fashion on the surface of the canvas, forming subtle contrasts in the way they are outlined against the neutral colour of the background. This effect is achieved with the truly expressive force characteristic of this artist's *oeuvre*. The scene is redolent of an almost extreme simplicity; this quality allows the viewer to experience directly the reality which confronts his eyes. In order to enhance a palpable sense of naturalism, Meléndez has suppressed any possible spatial relationships and only allows the solid base line, here exemplified by a simple and traditional, coarse-grained table constructed from planks, to obtrude; this magnifies the air of simplicity with which the whole composition is infused, and also prevents the spectator's attention from being distracted by extraneous details. Similar integrated groupings of bunches of grapes are also displayed in other canvases by Meléndez, both in the Prado Museum (see no. 939) and in other Spanish collections. There are also examples in certain foreign collections.

The appearance of the accumulated vine shoots, which rise to a considerable height, imbues them with the quality of a radial arrangement. This is a clear indication of the artist's perennial interest in stressing aspects of the composition which appear incidental, but in fact impose an intrinsic order, and serve as a balancing device to contrast with the two different types of grapes; the obvious and keen desire of the artist to impose an authentic sense of narrative on the composition results in levels of distinguished refinement unexpectedly reminiscent of precious jewellery. The technical virtuosity which Meléndez displays here confers the attributes of greatness on the overall ensemble; the sureness of the brushwork exudes a vivacity and supreme freshness of approach which could not be surpassed.

When including his signature in front of the table in the picture, the artist dispenses with the normal abbreviated form of his name and instead writes it out in full, along with the year of composition. These details unambiguously authenticate the picture, while also securely dating it. **J.J.L.**

17. Still Life with a Dish of Plums, Figs and Bread Roll

Oil on canvas: 41 x 62 cm
Signed on top of the napkin fold: L^{S}. M^{Z}
Madrid: Prado Museum, no. 905

Provenance
Royal Collections, Casita del Príncipe, El Escorial; Palacio Real de Aranjuez.

Bibliography
Soria, 1948, p. 216; Beltrán Martínez, 1964, no. 156; Tufts, 1971, p. 165; Luna, 1982-1983, p. 106, no. 31; Tufts, 1982, no. 4; Tufts, 1985a, pp. 77-80; Luna, 1995, p. 144; Cherry and Luna, 2004, p. 186, no. 16; Garrido and Cherry, 2004 [in print], no. 905.

Exhibitions
Caracas, 1981, no. 73; Madrid-Barcelona, 1982-1983, no. 31; Valencia, 1984, no. 25; Madrid, 2004, no. 16.

Over a flat surface (identical to most of the surfaces which Meléndez uses as supports in his still lifes) one can see a dish, decorated in the *castañuela* (castanet) style, with a painted border whose design was a popular feature of the time. The dish, possibly made in Talavera (Toledo), fulfils the rather inadequate function of container for a considerable quantity of plums – some still on their branches – which are piled on top. On one side, a ring-shaped roll of bread, placed over a folded napkin, reflects the impact of the light in a truly skilful way; on the other, three figs fill up the empty space on the left, seeking to balance the composition on both sides. The ring-shaped roll is a recurring feature in the *oeuvre* of Meléndez; examples can be seen in the Prado museum, the National Museum of Art in Catalonia, and in certain private collections.

This composition gives a shape and form to specific ideas which had been current in the Spanish pictorial tradition from the seventeenth century: the elements in the picture, exquisitely finished, are outlined against the dark neutral background; these are almost like set formulas designed to captivate the eye of the spectator. Also, the sense of order in which the verticals and horizontals are combined is very evident, in spite of the slight dislocation brought about by the series of diagonals which break up the tight-knit structural arrangement; however, this eccentricity serves to enhance the naturalism of the scene. All of this indicates a conscious analysis of the natural world on the part of the artist: his moulding of reality into, as it were, tactile shapes exudes a note of authenticity. The objects are thematically linked in subtle relationships, exemplifying the artist's refinement and his desire for a logical method of construction, which seeks both to achieve a sense of unity based on the harmonious combination of all the motifs, and to bring to fruition a truly realised integration of everything, in which no divisions are perceptible to the observer.

X-ray photography indicates that there were originally two further pieces of fruit in the bottom left-hand corner – between the figs and the small solitary plum on its branch, in the foreground. These fruits were of a discernibly different type from the varieties which dominate the completed canvas. **J.J.L.**

18. *Still Life with Apricots and Cherries*

Oil on Canvas: 41 x 62 cms.
Signed on the edge of the
table: Lᔆ. Mᶻ. ANO 1773.
Madrid. Prado Museum,
no. 920

Provenance
Royal Collections, Casita
del Príncipe, El Escorial;
Palacio Real de Aranjuez.

Bibliography
M. Soria, 1948, p. 217; E.
Tufts, 1971, p. 170; J.J. Luna,
1982-1983, p. 130, no. 43;
E. Tufts, 1982, no. 19; L.C.
Gutiérrez Alonso, 1983,
p. 166; E. Tufts, 1985,
pp. 84- 85. J.J. Luna, 1995,
p. 172; C. Garrido and P.
Cherry, 2004 (in print),
no. 920.

Exhibitions
Madrid-Barcelona, 1982-
1983, no. 43; Valencia, 1984,
no. 34; Raleigh-Dallas-
New York, 1985, no. 33.

Here, rising from a dish with a smooth and finely-decorated edge (probably crafted in Alcora, Buen Retiro in Madrid, or even possibly in the Orient) on which some finely-delineated linear motifs are just visible, a truly splendid cluster of apricots – some still on their branches, with their leaves shining brilliantly – makes a spectacular statement. The apricots are accompanied by a pile of cherries also on their branches: the entire ensemble is infused with a great sense of vitality and inventiveness, and displays the authentic quality of a decorative still life. Away from the dish, more apricots and cherries are dispersed over the surface of the table, which serves as the base line of the composition.

What is most outstanding in this work is the gracefulness and lightness which permeate the various structures; this approach differs considerably from the emphasis on solidity which had been the prominent characteristic of the artist's work in the 1760s. Here, the interplay of shape and line and also the fluency of the patterns suggest a palpable dynamism which is not often encountered in the artist's *oeuvre*. One is left with the impression that the elements in the picture, with their strong accent on liveliness and lack of proportion, are of a different aesthetic order from what one would expect of a still life. It looks as though the artist deliberately intended this; most likely, this was at the request of the royal patron who commissioned the work.

The overall conception is one of simplicity, even if some of the details are highly ornate. The decorative scheme is particularly successful, and all the individual minutiae are expressed with the artist's customary virtuosity. The diverse surface details of each object are superbly executed – ranging from roughness to smoothness, and differentiating dullness from a shiny brilliance, particularly where the fruits and leaves are concerned; the artist's intention is always to reproduce the tactile qualities of the materials and to offer to the spectator a *trompe l'oeil* sensation of verisimilitude. In an equally convincing manner, the table in the picture clearly displays the small grooves and fissures in the wood; there is a deliberate avoidance of the use of a glossy finish, the aim being to make the surface of the table as appropriately rough-hewn in appearance as possible. After all, the table is intended to look like an ordinary, domestic piece of furniture in frequent use.

It appears that this picture forms a pair with another work, catalogued as no. 921 in the Prado Museum. This conclusion, based purely on empirical evidence, is in accordance with the common features and analogous qualities which both canvases exhibit. Also, the two painting differ considerably from the usual practice of the artist: they lack the distinctive motifs and decorative effects which both enrich and add a level of complexity to most of the other still lifes by Meléndez. **J.J.L.**

19. Still Life with Apricots and Cherries

Oil on canvas, 37.5 x 50 cm.
Rosendo Naseiro Collection

Provenance
Private collection;
Rosendo Naseiro Collection.

Bibliography
Alcalá Subastas, *A la sombra de Goya. Pinturas y artes decorativas en colecciones particulares*, Madrid, 1999.

Exhibitions
Madrid, 1999, no. 37

This painting is a somewhat more simplified version of Meléndez's *Still Life with Apricots and Cherries* painted for the Prince of Asturias in 1773 (cat. 18). Meléndez's conception is the same in each picture; the main motif is an arrangement of apricots on a plate that is relieved by branches of fruit spreading outwards from the centre and further fruits arranged on the tabletop. However, close examination of the pictures reveals that Meléndez's variant is a combination of newly invented motifs, probably painted from life, and others recycled from the royal prototype. Meléndez has rearranged the apricots in the plate into a new configuration and has painted three new branches of fruit, laden with three, two and one apricot respectively. At the same time, the branch of apricots that extends outwards towards the upper left-hand corner of the picture is a simplified version of the same branch of fruit in the prototype, as is the branch of fruit that lies on the table at the right-hand side of the picture. Meléndez has, moreover, reduced the number of cherries to three and these occupy a similar position to those from which they have been copied in the royal prototype. Meléndez opted for a light grey background that he painted around the fruit and that lends itself to the luminous tonality of this particular work.

It is likely that this still life was painted at the same time as Meléndez's royal prototype of 1773 and certainly while the latter remained in his studio. The smaller dimensions of the picture relative to its prototype would explain Meléndez's reduction of the composition to its essentials and is further evidence of the care with which he composed the variations on his own still lifes. The painting is a prime example of Meléndez's technique of painting variants based on his own still lifes from the "master series" of works for the Prince of Asturias. As with the other autograph variants in this exhibition (cats 37, 38), it is impossible to tell merely from looking which of the motifs have been recycled from other pictures and those which are likely to have been freshly observed from nature. **P.C.**

20. Still Life with Dish of Figs, Bottle and Loaf of Bread

Oil on canvas: 34.5 x 48 cm
Signed: L^S. M^Z. D. R. D^{ZO}.
I. S^{to}. P^e. 1771
Madrid: El Escorial,
Casita del Príncipe
(Patrimonio Nacional)

Provenance
Royal Collections, Casita
del Príncipe, El Escorial;
Palacio Real de Aranjuez.

Bibliography
Thieme-Becker xxiv, 1930,
p. 361; Tufts, 1971, p. 192;
Benezit, 1999, vi, p. 330;
Luna, 1982-1983, p. 114,
no. 35; Tufts, 1982, no. 72;
Gutiérrez Alonso, 1983,
p. 165; Tufts, 1985a, p. 75;
Luna, 1995, p. 126; Cherry
and Luna, 2004, p. 188,
no. 17.

Exhibitions
Madrid-Barcelona, 1982-
1983, no. 35; Madrid, 2004,
no. 17.

The artistic method of Meléndez always involves, firstly, the suitable and judicious arrangement of the chosen objects on the canvas, followed by the painstaking task of unifying and integrating all of the elements in a flexible and apparently effortless way; thus, the diverse textures and surface details of dissimilar objects are correspondingly rendered and conveyed in a manner befitting the context. Here, for instance, the polished smooth surface of the bottle is sharply differentiated from the rugged and irregular contours of the figs. The luminous effects of the radiating light confer a special quality of enhanced meaning on the picture. The diverse elements grouped together, receiving the impact of the rays of light from the left-hand side, are highlighted in a pronounced way, in accordance with their arrangement and in keeping with the individual differences of textures.

A considerable number of black figs, each one juxtaposed against its companion, are piled high on a dish decorated in the *castañuela* (castanet) style. The surface of the dish is half-covered in fig leaves, accompanied by still more leaves which create unusual and rather whimsical shapes as they curl back against each other; in the middle distance, at one side, a large loaf of bread is sharply distinguished, both by its colour and the uneven ridges of its surface, from the dark bottle alongside, which is firmly integrated into the composition. Just as in other canvases by the artist, the underlying linear structures serve as an integrating principle, imparting a sense of tense repose to the scene.

X-ray photography has revealed that the artist had originally painted a piece of cheese, or something very similar, within the lower left-hand corner of the picture.

In this densely-filled composition, the harmonious tonalities display subtle characteristics and features to a greater extent than in other works by this artist: yellows, greens and blacks, which together combine the chromatic individualities of the loaf, the leaves and the bottle, are set against the roseate values of the interior sections of the figs and also against the purple and iridescent hues of their skins. The colouristic medley is an indication of the artist's consummate flair for the creation of hues, tints and shades which are totally in keeping with what is required – including the evocation of a tactile dimension. J.J.L.

21. Still Life with Bread, Pomegranates, Figs, Bottle and Wine Glass

Oil on Canvas: 36 x 49 cms.
Signed on the edge of the
table: E⁰. L^Z. M^Z. D. R^a. D⁰.
IS^{to}. P^e. AÑO 1770.
Madrid. Prado Museum,
no. 937

Provenance
Royal Collections, Casita
del Príncipe, El Escorial;
Palacio Real de Aranjuez.

Bibliography
E. Lafuente Ferrari, 1935,
p. 169; M. Soria, 1948, p. 217;
F.J. Sánchez Cantón, 1965,
fig. 221; E. Tufts, 1971, p. 176;
J.J. Luna, 1982-1983, p. 84,
no. 20; E. Tufts, 1982, no. 36;
L.C. Gutiérrez Alonso, 1983,
p. 165; E. Tufts, 1985, p. 71,
72; J.J. Luna, 1995, p. 110;
C. Garrido and P. Cherry,
2004 (in print), no. 937.

Exhibitions
London, 1954-1955, no. 16;
London, 1972, no. 191;
Madrid-Barcelona, 1982-
1983, no. 20; Valencia,
1984, no. 17.

The artist displays, on a smooth and even surface, certain varied and distinctive motifs which, taken together, make up both the ingredients for a dessert and its accompanying dessert service. In the foreground, the knife and the napkin are duly prominent; on top of the napkin, a loaf of bread shines with reflected light as is also the case with the earthenware or metal dish which contains figs and pomegranates: these fruits are arranged in diverse ways to avoid monotony. A stray fig (which has fallen from the dish) together with the knife impart a quality of spatial depth to this section of the picture; the artistic delineation and positioning of the knife recall Dutch still lifes from the seventeenth century. At the same level, but farther back in the composition, a large wine glass and wine bottle rise up, in the manner of presiding watchtowers. Their presence affirms their status as pronounced vertical structures, balancing out the implicitly orthogonal scheme of the composition. The bottle and glass were most likely produced at the Royal Factory in La Granja: this view is also expressed by L.C. Gutiérrez Alonso.

As usual, the artist's principal aim is the authentic reproduction of the qualities and shapes of the objects depicted. The surfaces of the wineglass and the bottle are executed in a very skilful way; in the case of the bottle, there are discernible reflections in the glass, in which parts of the room not otherwise documented, are displayed: a window is visible as well as the roof structure, and details of the rafters.

Thanks to the precision and technical flair of Meléndez, such detailed observation serves not only as testimony to his skill with the paintbrush, but also as confirmation of his consummate expertise. Thus, at one and the same time, mass and volume are successfully conveyed while two sources of light are also appropriately established. Because these two light sources are almost imperceptible, they constitute an aesthetic principle of the first order, thus eluding the danger of monotony.

By its appearance next to the artist's signature, the year 1770 would appear to be the date of composition; however, E. Tufts dissents from this view. Undoubtedly, the canvas belongs to this period of the artist's creativity, judging by the stylistic criteria: the work is much more decorative that the severely plain nature of the still lifes executed by Meléndez in the 1760s. Intriguingly, he includes here, beside the dish of figs, other objects which do not strictly fit the description of kitchen crockery. In addition to this, one can see reflected in the bottle, as if in a mirror, a shadow which could well be a portrait of the artist in front of his easel; this attractive feature is characteristic of many Dutch and Flemish still lifes. Meléndez would have studied some of these, with the aim of securing for his own work the beauty and refinement of their artistic resources. **J.J.L.**

22. Still Life with Plums, Figs, Bread, a Keg, Jug, and Kitchen Utensils

Oil on canvas: 35 x 48 cm
Signed on the edge of
the table: L.M^z.
Madrid: Prado Museum,
no. 924

Provenance
Royal Collections, Casita
del Príncipe, El Escorial;
Palacio Real de Aranjuez.

Bibliography
Soria, 1948, p. 217; Lastic,
1955, p. 41; Lastic, 1955, no.
9, p. 21; Chueca Goitia, 1958,
fig. 163; Sánchez Cantón,
1965, fig. 210; Sánchez
Palacios, 1965, p. 40; Tufts,
1971, p. 171; Aparicio, 1973,
p. 17; Luna, 1982-1983, p. 76,
no. 16; Tufts, 1982, no. 23;
Gutiérrez Alonso, 1983,
p. 165; Pérez Sánchez, 1983-
1984, p. 165, no. 148; Tufts,
1985a, pp. 68-69; Luna,
1995, p. 86; Luna and
Cherry, 2004, p. 168, no. 7;
Garrido and Cherry, 2004
[in print], no. 924.

Exhibitions
London, 1954-1955, no. 14;
Stockholm, 1959-1960, no.
72; Madrid-Barcelona, 1982-
1983, no. 16; Madrid, 1983-
1984, no. 148; Valencia, 1984,
no. 14; Raleigh-Dallas-New
York, 1985, no. 15; Paris,
1987-1988, no. 84; London,
1989, no. 19; Geneva, 1989,
no. 55; Madrid, 1989-1990,
no. 68; Madrid, 2004, no. 7.

This picture contains a compendium of the objects and motifs most frequently encountered in the *oeuvre* of Meléndez; apart from the intrinsic artistic merit, the effect is one of breathtaking verisimilitude, and its documentary value is also of great importance. Set down on a table of the type habitually used by Meléndez — fashioned from a series of planks, in which the grains and knots of wood stand out — and positioned between a group of plums and some black figs, a loaf of bread and a large *jarra de bola* (a round-shaped jug) make a grand statement. The jug is typical of the ware produced in Talavera de la Reina (Toledo) and at Puente del Arzobispo, and is white in colour with a decorated stripe of yellow ochre, reflecting the use of antimony as an alloy; the handle twists upwards and inwards, in the manner of a Solomonic pillar (a characteristic feature of eighteenth century sculpture and decoration). Behind the jug, several decorated china plates are visible, the decorations being of the types known as *rosilla* (little rose) and *adormidera* (referring to the opium poppy). A keg for holding syrup or jam, and a bowl of Alcorcón manufacture, within which a fish is displayed, complete the background. The ample and varied resources on show give the composition

a distinct appearance — quite different from the conventional and repetitive nature of the utensils and typical foods presented to the spectator's gaze in other canvases; the picture also acquires a quality of special significance, without failing to convince the viewer of the veristic values characteristic of the genre.

The linking of the vertical and horizontal planes is totally assured and manages to convey a palpable sense of space with great facility; also, the play of light is effected in a masterly way with thick brushstrokes applied over the various surfaces, conferring the illusion of high relief on the assembled objects while also particularising each one of them. The diverse shapes and volumes truly stand out, bathed as they are in the diffuse and carefully contrived luminous effects which immerse the overall composition. Delicate spots of still brighter light punctuate the canvas at several points, serving to highlight the diverse outlines, maximise the illusion of volumes and make the transition from light to shadow more dramatic. The contrasts of tonalities and colouristic effects enrich the composition immeasurably, endowing the whole schema with an enlivening agility, without any trace of awkward transitions or stodginess. **J.J.L.**

23. *Still Life with a Plate of Azeroles, Apples, Pears, Cheese and Kitchen Utensils*

Oil on Canvas: 40 x 62 cms
Signed on the box:
L^S. M^Z. 1771
Madrid. Prado Museum, no. 909

Provenance
Royal Collections, Casita del Príncipe, El Escorial; Palacio Real de Aranjuez.

Bibliography
M. Soria, 1948, p. 216; E. Tufts, 1971, p. 167; J.J. Luna, 1982-1983, p. 108, no. 32; E. Tufts, 1982, no. 8; L.C. Gutiérrez Alonso, 1983, p. 166; E. Tufts, 1985, pp. 73-74 ; A.E. Pérez Sánchez, 1987, pp. 186-189 ; J.A. Tomlinson, 1990, p. 87; J.J. Luna, 1995, p. 118; C. Garrido and P. Cherry, 2004 (in print), no. 909.

Exhibitions
Bordeaux-Paris-Madrid, 1979-1980 (Spanish edition) no. 39; Belgrade, 1981, no. 28; Munich-Vienna, 1982, no. 46; Madrid-Barcelona, 1982-1983, no. 32; Valencia, 1984, no. 26; Madrid, 1988-1989, no. 68; London, 1995, no. 56; Madrid, 1995, no. 27.

This work displays the usual characteristics one comes to expect of Meléndez: a rigorously exact observation of surrounding reality and the use of skilful effects — each complementing the other — which show evidence of having been progressively painted onto the canvas in three stages, i.e. during the preliminary sketches, at a later developmental stage of the project, and as final finishing touches. A considerable number of widely diverse motifs are combined in the composition, with the obvious aim of providing formal contrasts between the elements, and of imposing a unifying principle of compositional harmony on the overall ensemble. This sense of harmony particularly distinguishes the work.

An earthenware dish, with undulating edges and heaped high with azeroles, forms the central element in the composition, due to its positioning and also because of its distinctive colour. A section of cheese which appears to be fresh is situated on one side of the dish; two apples and a pear are located on the other. In the middle ground, a bottle of wine serves to demarcate the vertical axis of the surrounding area. The bottle is flanked by a glazed earthenware jar and by a honey jar made in Marises, whose workmanship reflects eighteenth century canons of taste in that it is finely embellished with gold; it also bears the decorative motif known as *sarta de riñones* (i.e. a series of kidney-shaped motifs). The background is occupied by a keg (which probably functions as a receptacle for preserves or syrup) and also some containers of sweets in boxes of different shapes.

The picture is proof positive of the artist's facility with regard to the integration of different colours into a unitary scheme. Meléndez experimented with special colour-istic effects with the aim of infusing the volumes and forms with a realised sense of solidity, and to reproduce a palpable quality of space between and surrounding the depicted objects. It was his clear intention to create three-dimensionality by outlining and silhouetting some of the elements over others, and by highlighting the objects farther back in the picture against the neutral background: the latter covers much of the upper half of the composition completely. Also, the carefully contrived luminous effects demarcate the surface details of the pictorial elements, and also enhance the individual characteristics of the objects to consummate effect.

A copy of this picture exists in a private collection in Madrid: the components of the original canvas, along with their arrangement, are exactly reproduced, and the dimensions of both paintings are identical. There is yet another copy of the original work, currently in the possession of the Marquises of Tamarón (in Castillo de Arcos de la Erontera, in the province of Cadiz). However, this particular copy, even though the general scheme and particular details of the original are reproduced, appears to be an inferior work, and its authorship is uncertain. **J.J.L.**

24. Still Life with Limes, Box of Jelly, Butterfly and Kitchen Utensils

Oil on canvas: 35 x 48 cm
Signed on the edge of the
table:L.M^{z}
Madrid: Prado Museum,
no. 925

Provenance
Royal Collections, Casita
del Príncipe, El Escorial;
Palacio Real de Aranjuez.

Bibliography
Soria, 1948, p. 217; Tufts,
1971, p. 172; Luna, 1982-
1983, p. 78, no. 17; Tufts,
1982, no. 24; Gutiérrez
Alonso, 1983, p. 165; Pérez
Sánchez, 1983-1984, p. 162,
no. 145; Tufts, 1985a, p. 70;
Pérez Sánchez, 1987, p. 188;
Luna, 1994a, pp. 538-539;
Luna, 1995, p. 104; Cherry
and Luna, 2004, p. 192,
no. 19; Garrido and Cherry,
2004 [in print], no. 925.

Exhibitions
Madrid-Barcelona, 1982-
1983, no. 17; Madrid, 1983-
1984, no. 145; Madrid, 2004,
no. 19.

A considerable number of limes are grouped together in the foreground in the seemingly artless disorder which is a characteristic of the artist's method; the limes occupy almost half of the painted area of the picture. Behind the fruit stands a glazed earthenware jar of honey – like those which were manufactured in Biar (Alicante) and Lucena (Córdoba) for common use. This jar is covered in a green glaze made from copper oxide and shows definite signs, judging by its contours, of the firing process used in its fabrication; the depiction is typical of the artist's virtuosity and precision in detail. In the background, an open box of jelly can be seen: it rests on a dish with corrugated edges and decorated in the so-called *castañuela* (castanet) style. Alongside it stands a silver or pewter salver which serves as a base for a highly decorated cup. A butterfly which flies over the assembled objects is an interesting feature because of its rarity in such compositions; however, the quality of its workmanship is mediocre. The butterfly's presence is noteworthy, but lacks a sense of authenticity. The insect is poorly executed and no real sense of naturalism is evoked.

Upon analysing the arresting china cup which rises above the rest of the objects in the picture – by its position, making the fruit the central element of the work – one can immediately see that it is of Mexican provenance (more precisely, from Guadalajara), of the type known as Tonalá, because of its place of manufacture. There were many such decorated pieces in Spain and, in particular, at the royal court in Madrid; the brisk trade in such sumptuous objects from beyond the Atlantic Ocean is well-attested during the eighteenth century. Valuable china and crockery were being shipped at this time from Mexico to grace the tables of aristocratic patrons in Spain – especially those aristocrats with family connections among the ruling elite at the viceregal court of New Spain, in Mexico City.
J.J.L.

25. Still Life with Box of Jelly, Bread, Salver, Glass and Winecooler

Oil on Canvas: 49 x 37 cms.
Signed on the edge of the
table: E^g. L^s. M^z. R^a. D^o.
IS^o. P^e. 1770.
Madrid. Prado Museum,
no. 906

Provenance
Royal Collections, Casita
del Príncipe, El Escorial;
Palacio Real de Aranjuez.

Bibliography
M. Soria, 1948, p. 216; G.
Kelly, 1955, p. 99; V. Young,
1960, p. 48; E. Tufts, 1971,
p. 166; E. Tufts, 1977, p. 142;
J.J. Luna, 1982-1983, p. 88,
no. 22; E. Tufts, 1982, no. 5;
L.C. Gutiérrez Alonso, 1983,
p. 165; A.E. Pérez Sánchez,
1983-1984, p. 164, no. 147; E.
Tufts, 1985, p. 73; J.J. Luna,
1995, p. 114; C. Garrido and
P. Cherry, 2004 (in print),
no. 906.

Exhibitions
London, 1954-1955, no. 11;
Stockholm, 1959-1960,
no. 71; Madrid-Barcelona,
1982-1983, no. 22; Madrid,
1983-1984, no. 147; Valencia,
1984, no. 19; Raleigh-Dallas-
New York, 1985, no. 17;
London, 1989, no. 18; Bilbao,
1999-2000, no. 41; Río de
Janeiro, 2002.

In spite of Meléndez's perennial interest in ordinary, everyday scenarios – exemplified in the way objects are placed in the foreground to catch the eye of the spectator, and also by his habit of including ordinary foodstuffs and commonplace utensils in his work – there are occasions when Meléndez inserts more opulent and highly decorated objects which would not normally be found on a conventional kitchen table. This is the case here; in this composition, an elegant silver salver functions as a pedestal for a glass fashioned from lead crystal: this glass reflects the light in a gleaming and sparkling way that is carefully worked out with geometric precision. Beside it – also apparently made from lead crystal – a fork, pointing diagonally towards the background, and a dish with an undulating border both enrich the composition to an even greater degree. On top of the dish, a box of sweet jelly is positioned: the lid of the box has been removed and the jelly reflects the mirror image of a ring-shaped roll of bread, which is perched on a wrinkled napkin. The scene is completed by the inclusion of a bulky wine cooler, from which emerges the crystal neck of a bottle of wine. The bottle itself constitutes an elegant vertical structure; its linear surfaces reflect the light beautifully, and the thin rope covering which surrounds the bottle's contours – right up to the cork – is vividly realised in a skillfully serpentine way.

When compared with other still lifes by Meléndez, this canvas is more refined, due perhaps to the elegant character of the objects on display; the various elements, which together make up the ingredients of an appetizing dessert, are assembled in a truly magisterial way. The fact that 1770 was the year of composition – this is documented by the artist himself – allows us to make comparisons with other pictures by Meléndez which share stylistic similarities but whose dates of composition are not securely known. One example of such a picture with which this work shares many affinities is one of the two vertical canvases on view in the Museo Nacional d'Art de Catalunya.

From the technical point of view, the painting reaches the *summum bonum* of virtuosity; this appears to have been achieved through the studied co-ordination of all the elements: a richness of detail is aimed at, along with a perfect balance of shapes and volumes. These are the qualities which make this canvas stand out from the rest of the artist's *oeuvre*. In addition, the use of a judicious *chiaroscuro*, which sets off the different sections of the composition, serves to reinforce the desired illusion of verisimilitude; the play of light is also an important factor. **J.J.L.**

26. Still Life with Chocolate Service and Bread Rolls

Oil on canvas: 50 x 37.5 cm
Signed on the edge of the
table: E. Lˢ. Mᶻ. Dᴼ. ISᴼ.
P. 1770
Madrid: Prado Museum,
no. 929

Provenance
Royal Collections, Casita
del Príncipe, El Escorial;
Palacio Real de Aranjuez.

Bibliography
Aguilera, 1946, lám. xii;
Soria, 1948, p. 217;
Enciclopedia, n.d., xxxiv,
p. 640; Sánchez Cantón,
1965, fig. 209; Pignatti,
1966, fig. 10; Tufts, 1971,
p. 173; Tufts, 1974, lám. 7;
Bergström, 1977, p. 202;
Luna, 1982-1983, p. 86,
no. 21; Tufts, 1982, no. 28;
Gutiérrez Alonso, 1983,
pp. 163, 165; Tufts, 1985a,
pp. 72-73; Moulin, 1989,
p. 344; Luna, 1994a, p. 38;
Luna, 1995, p. 112; Cherry
and Luna, 2004, p. 194,
no. 20;Garrido and Cherry,
2004 [in print], no. 929.

Exhibitions
Las Palmas de Gran
Canaria, 1973, no. 26;
Madrid-Barcelona, 1982-
1983, no. 21; Valencia, 1984,
no. 18; Raleigh-Dallas-New
York, 1985, no. 16; Florence,
1986, no. 78; London, 1989,
no. 17; Madrid, 1995,
no. 28; Madrid, 1997, xi, 9;
Frankfurt, 1999-2000, no.
104; Madrid, 2004, no. 20.

While one can say that, as a general rule, Meléndez, in his canvases, used objects which were commonly found in Spain at the time, this work is the exception which confirms the rule. Among the different motifs in the picture there is a small cup, displaying a polychrome vegetable pattern of decoration; this object appears not to be of Spanish manufacture, but of oriental origin. The cup, with its accompanying plate, appears to be of porcelain and Cantonese in origin; it is likely to be a product of the Ching dynasty and was probably secured as part of a Spanish colonial trade mission.

The canvas displays a sumptuous chocolate service: a large copper chocolate pot combines emphases on verticality and horizontality, with its tall chocolate grinder and its long handle; in front of the pot, a large plate contains the delicate cup, a bread roll, and some pieces of sponge cake. One piece of the cake lies on the table itself in the foreground, along with some round tablets of chocolate which have spilled out from the original wrapping paper.

"During the eighteenth century, two types of hot drinks were particularly favoured in Spain: drinking chocolate and coffee.

Coffee was more to the taste of French people and was also greatly preferred by certain Spaniards; hot chocolate, on the other hand, had become an institution in Spain, retaining the great popularity it had enjoyed during the seventeenth century. King Charles III of Spain, in spite of his French ancestry and his long residency in Italy, was fond of his cup of chocolate, often requesting a second cup. The chocolate pot in common use at the royal palace was immensely large and was obviously intended for the benefit of a considerable number of people" (J.A. Crow, *Spain*, New York, 1963). The great predilection for hot chocolate in Spain explains the inclusion of the chocolate service here, as well as the accompanying sweet confectionery; sweet snacks of this kind, known as *meriendas* (the Spanish equivalent of afternoon tea) frequently appear in this artist's *oeuvre*. However, apart from these considerations, this particular canvas elicits an undeniable level of originality with regard to the way the ensemble is structured, and also because of the unusual motifs which, in combination, inspire the scene with an almost palpable reality. **J.J.L.**

27. Still Life with Watermelons and Apples in a Landscape

Oil on canvas: 63 x 84 cm
Signed on the stone:
L.^{S}.E^g.M^z.D^o. AÑO 1771
Madrid: Prado Museum,
no. 923

Provenance
Royal Collections, Casita
del Príncipe, El Escorial;
Palacio Real de Aranjuez.

Bibliography
Soria, 1948, p. 217; Tufts,
1971, p. 171; Luna, 1982-
1983, p. 98, no. 27; Tufts,
1982, no. 22; Pérez Sánchez,
1983-1984, p. 167, no. 150;
Tufts, 1985a, pp. 77-78;
Luna, 1995, p. 138; Cherry
and Luna, 2004, p. 200,
no. 23; Garrido and Cherry,
2004 [in print], no. 923.

Exhibitions
Madrid-Barcelona, 1982-
1983, no. 27; Madrid, 1983-
1984, no. 150; Stockholm,
1995, no. 170; Madrid, 2004,
no. 23.

The watermelons which appear in the foreground project themselves, as it were, at the spectator with an expressive force that can hardly be equalled. As well as an attractive quality of freshness, and an outstanding sense of sober plasticity, the picture, composed with restraint, displays an assurance of execution which allows the viewer to observe the virtuosity of the artist: the solidity of the design, the rich texture of the colour-scheme and the perfect representation of reality, even down to the tiniest details.

The arrangement of the splendid orchard fruits is distinctly methodical, without seeking to be decorative in a conventional and facile way; a concrete sense of painstaking exactitude exerts its own primacy, which is further highlighted by the subtle contrast of light and shadow. Meléndez, who usually depicts neutral backgrounds without the inclusion of specific details, here, for once, includes a precisely-defined landscape as a background. This, an original feature, also recalls the panoramas painted on the beautiful pages of the choir books in the Royal Chapel in Madrid: Meléndez also illustrated a number of these, using similar formulas. Here, the unusual grouping of the elements and the fact that an open-air scene is realistically evoked remind the viewer of a typical Neapolitan still life: the aesthetic similarity is undeniable. Most likely, Meléndez was influenced by pictures he viewed during his sojourn in Italy, but he also had access to still lifes of the Neapolitan school in Madrid.

This picture appears to be a companion to the canvas which immediately follows it in the catalogue (cat. 28), a work (also in the Prado Museum) with which it shares thematic associations and certain affinities with regard to dimensions: both canvases display fruits in the foreground and landscapes at the back. In both cases, ripe pears and luxuriantly luscious larger fruits are juxtaposed — their fecundity designed to delight the beholder. In view of all this, both pictures were probably painted in 1771. The melon as a motif, whether intact or cut in sections, is also celebrated in a few other works by the artist — now in various Spanish and foreign collections.

In accordance with X-ray findings, we can now confirm that the canvas was re-used by the artist, because beneath the existing pigments another composition (mostly of vegetation and large leaves) is discernible. **J.J.L.**

28. Still Life with Pomegranates, Apples, Azaroles and Grapes in a Landscape

Oil on canvas: 62.5 x 84 cm
Signed on the stone:
L⁵.Eº.Mᶻ.Dᶻº. AÑO 1771
Madrid: Prado Museum,
no. 922

Provenance
Royal Collections, Casita del Príncipe, El Escorial; Palacio Real de Aranjuez.

Bibliography
Soria, 1948, p. 217; Tufts, 1971, p. 171; Luna, 1982-1983, p. 96, no. 26; Tufts, 1982, no. 21; Tufts, 1985a, p. 77; Luna, 1995, p. 156; Cherry and Luna, 2004, p. 201, no. 24; Garrido and Cherry, 2004 [in print], no. 922.

Exhibitions
Madrid-Barcelona, 1982-1983, no. 26; Valencia, 1984, no. 21; Raleigh-Dallas-New York, 1985, no. 18; Madrid, 2004, no. 24.

Meléndez has managed, with considerable skill, to combine different species of fruit in an apparently disorganised association, while in fact integrating them in an harmonious combination. The truly spectacular open pomegranates, displaying the fecundity of their transparent seeds, are placed together with grapes, pears and cherries, forming one united theme. The structure of the composition is achieved in a ground-breaking way, full advantage being taken of the uneven terrain to avail of an effect of terraced gradients; thus, the composition is in the shape of a triangle, the base being a stone embankment with irregular and broken edges instead of a wooden table. In accordance with his usual practice, Meléndez has included his name and the date of composition in the foreground. The particular locale chosen as a background is an open-air scene in the countryside; the bushes and shrubs in semi-darkness stand out, silhouetted against a cloudy sky.

This is a companion piece to the last-mentioned work (cat. 27) with which it bears an obvious relationship in composition and in the dimensions of the fruits; in both works, the diagonal lines which define the upper sections of the canvases are emphasised, the overall structure being in the shape of a V. The form and position of the signature and date are also analogous, as is also the general concept of the paintings, both of which also evoke other thematic parallels. If, in this particular work, the pomegranates occupy pride of place whereas, in the other, watermelons play the leading role, there is nevertheless an obvious similarity in the way that the smaller fruits occupy symmetrically subordinate positions. J.J.L.

29. Still Life with Plums and Blackberries

30. Still Life with Strawberries

Oil on canvas, 37 x 50 cm.
Signed: L.ˢ M.ᶻ D.ᶻᵒ
Private collection

Oil on canvas, 37 x 50 cm.
Private Collection

Provenance
Both Private collection,
Madrid; Private collection,
Geneva; Private collection.

Bibliography
Luna, 1989, pp. 373-4;
Luna, 1995, nos. 48 and 46
respectively; Jordan, 1997,
nos. 18 and 19 respectively;
Cherry and Luna, 2004,
pp. 204-206, nos. 25 and 26.

Exhibitions
Madrid, 2004, nos. 25
and 26.

Meléndez varied his artistic repertoire by painting still lifes in a landscape, whose format derived ultimately from a type of painting that had become popular in Italy in the previous century. The attraction of these works lay in the combination of still life and landscape, and in showing the depicted fruits in their natural element. The evident success of the four large landscape format still lifes that Meléndez painted for the Prince of Asturias (cats 27, 28) may have inspired him to paint similar works for private clients. This is shown by the three paintings exhibited here that are close in type to Meléndez's royal paintings, although smaller in scale and with fewer elements. In fact, these paintings are of an equivalent size to Meléndez's small horizontal format kitchen still lifes (cat. 24)

One of the pictures shows an arrangement of green plums and a bowl of blackberries, and the other a wild strawberry patch, with a basket of freshly picked strawberries. The butterfly appears to be of the *Abraxas grossulariata* species, that is found in parts of the Sierra de Guadarrama. Although butterflies are unusual motifs in Meléndez's still lifes, these are common in other schools of painting and in flower pictures. The short-lived beauty of butterflies lent itself to symbolic interpretation in Northern still life painting of the seventeenth century, where these could signify the transience of life itself and cause viewers to contemplate their afterlife. However, Meléndez's objectively naturalistic still lifes do not seem to be impregnated with any such transcendental symbolism. The presence of the insect in this particular work may be explained in rather more literal terms, having been attracted to the fruit on a summer's day. In this way, the butterfly is a piece of pictorial rhetoric and a means of demonstrating to the viewer the freshness and aroma of the fruit, that has been recently picked, judging from the fact that some fruits are shown still on the branch.

Despite being staged in open-air settings, the compositions of these paintings differ little from Meléndez's still lifes on a table top. The fruits are shown against a pleasant, verdant landscape backdrop, laid out for the viewer on an earthen ledge reminiscent of the tabletop in Meléndez's interior still lifes. Moreover, the pictures maintain the same low viewpoint as these, as can be seen in the emphatic perspective of the bowl of blackberries, and the fruits gain in monumentality against the low horizon of the distant landscape. A raised shelf of earth was a useful pictorial recourse that allowed Meléndez to place objects at a higher level

in the middle ground of the painting. While Meléndez's pictorial stagecraft would be puzzling in realistic terms, perhaps, however, some form of open-air meal is suggested here, since the blackberries and strawberries are presented in a bowl and a basket respectively. These motifs appear in another Meléndez landscape format still life in this exhibition (cat. 31) and a painting in Stockholm (fig. 65).

Another evident pictorial device in the pictures is the profile of the landscape features, that fall in a diagonal accent from one side of the picture to the other. This is effective in closing off the distance and maintaining attention on the motifs in the foreground. In paired paintings, such as the present pair, and those from the royal series (cats 27, 28), the asymmetry of one picture was resolved in a symmetrical balance with its pendant, whose landscape falls in a contrary direction. **P.C.**

Fig. 65: Luis Meléndez, *Still Life with a Basket of Strawberries in a Landscape*
Oil on canvas, 36,5 x 59,5 cm
Stockholm, National Museum

31. Still Life with Hazelnuts, Azeroles and Blackberries

Oil on canvas, 37.5 x 49.5 cm.
Signed: L. M.
Rosendo Naseiro collection

Provenance
Private collection; Rosendo
Naseiro collection.

Bibliography
Luna, 1989, pp. 373-5;
Cherry and Luna, 2004,
p. 208, no. 27.

Exhibitions
Madrid, 2004, no. 27.

There are evident similarities between this painting and *Still Life with Plums and Blackberries* (cat. 29) in terms of the subject matter of blackberries and the painting's composition and size. Azeroles were commonly consumed fruits in the eighteenth century and appear in other still lifes by Meléndez (cats 23, 28). The hazelnuts, however, are a unique motif in Meléndez's known still lifes; these appear freshly picked and are still in their leafy husks, that curl and flare with natural vitality and are painted with a spontaneous touch. The air of naturalness implied by the apparently haphazard arrangement of fruits on the ground, as if lying where these have fallen from their trees, is belied by the picked blackberries in the bowl, that are evidently presented to the viewer ready for their consumption in an open-air meal. The dark landscape mass falls in a diagonal accent towards the right-hand side of the composition and is counterbalanced by the bright colour accents of the fruit and a luminous patch of blue sky. The fruit is depicted in close up in the foreground plane of the picture and daringly juxtaposed with a distant landscape vista, whose recession is checked by a screening broken tree. Sunlight catching the edges of leaves and clouds evokes the freshness of a summer's day in this work, one of the most attractive Meléndez's small landscape format still lifes. **P.C.**

32. Still Life with Fruit, Bread and Jugs

Oil on canvas, 51 x 74 cm.
Signed: Luis Menendez
de Rivera Durazo
Barcelona, Museu Nacional
d'Art de Catalunya
no. 24.246.

Provenance
Leopoldo Gil collection,
Barcelona; 1922 deposited
in the Museo de Bellas Artes
de Cataluña and acquired
in 1944.

Bibliography
Tufts, 1985, no. 52; Luna,
1995, no. 39; Cherry and
Luna, 2004, p. 210, no. 28.

Exhibitions
Raleigh-Dallas-New York,
1985, no. 21; Madrid, 2004,
no. 28.

Fruit is the main motif in this densely composed still life, comprising apples, black and white grapes, and three melons. The latter fruits are tied with the strings with which the fruit was customarily suspended in a dark, cool place in order to preserve it fresh during the winter months. The "movement" of the knotted strings and the curling vine tendrils and leaves enliven considerably the upper part of the picture. For the rest, Meléndez has drawn on a familiar repertoire of objects. The plain Talavera jug with a twisted handle is the same as that which appears in *Still Life with Plums, Figs, Bread, a Keg, Jug and Kitchen Utensils* (cat. 22). The wine bottle and terracotta jug are of a type seen in other paintings, such as *Still Life with Pears, Wine and Basket* (cat. 33) and *Still Life with Oranges, Walnuts and Boxes of Sweetmeats* (cat. 34). In a remarkable passage of close observation, a high window in the room in which Meléndez painted the picture is reflected in the glass wine bottle, whose body also reflects the red blush of the apple beside it. The loaf of bread on the napkin in the foreground shows Meléndez's habitual concern for the detailed representation of the formal and textural intricacies of its crust. The picture is unusual for being signed with Meléndez's full name and, although this is discretely placed in the shaded part of the table edge, it is directly below the loaf of bread, a leitmotif in his work and a tour de force of his representational ability. **P.C.**

33. Still Life with Pears, Wine and Basket

Oil on canvas, 61 x 81 cm.
Signed in black on the
basket: L. M.ᶻ
New York, Private collection

Provenance
Salvador Mesquita, Buenos
Aires (until 1968); Berlini
collection, Lausanne;
Matthiesen Fine Art Ltd.,
London, 1985 (from whom
acquired by the present
owner).

Bibliography
London, National Gallery,
1989, p. 84, no. 24; Luna,
1989, pp. 370-2; London,
1997, pp. 131-6, no.17 A;
Cherry and Luna, 2004,
p. 212, no. 29.

Exhibitions
London, National Gallery,
1989, no. 24; London, 1997,
no.17 A; Madrid, 2004,
no. 29.

An arrangement of luminous and warmly coloured fruit, comprising pears, peaches and a small bunch of green grapes, form the predominant motifs in the foreground of this still life. Behind the fruit are arranged a wine cooler and bottle of wine, and a basket with a white cloth in it, all of which are motifs familiar from other works by Meléndez. The relatively straightforward composition is deeply satisfying in terms of its formal relationships. The success of this also depends, of course, on the artist's skill in capturing the range of colours and textures of the things that he was so used to painting.

The small bunch of grapes at the right-hand corner of the composition appears to have been a late addition, since these show the pears and tabletop beneath, due to the increased transparency of the pigments over time. They were probably added when the main features were finished, for reasons of chromatic balance. Finishing touches such as these are not uncommon in Meléndez's paintings and ensured pictorial coherence, above and beyond any arrangement of forms that actually existed in front of the artist.

From stylistic evidence, the picture would appear to date from the same time as *Still Life with Melon, Pears and a Basket of Bread* (fig. 61), a work of approximately the same size. The shared provenance of this still life and *Still Life with Oranges, Walnuts and Boxes of Sweetmeats* (cat. 34) shows that these paintings were paired in the past. Both paintings depict fruit and their compositions are sympathetic to one another, although without any obvious sense of complementarity. They are painted on canvases of the same size and type. However, technical examination of this painting shows no compositional changes or unusual features beneath the paint surface comparable with the surprise found in its supposed pendant. **P.C.**

34. *Still Life with Oranges, Walnuts and Boxes of Sweetmeats*

Oil on canvas, 61 x 81 cms.
Signed: L^S E^O M^Z D^. /
ANO 1772.
London, The National
Gallery, no. NG 6505

Provenance
Salvador Mesquita, Buenos
Aires (until 1968); Berlini
collection, Lausanne;
Matthiesen Fine Art Ltd.,
London, 1986 (from whom
acquired by the present
owner).

Bibliography
Levey, 1987, p. 192; Luna,
1989, pp. 370-2; London,
National Gallery, 1989, p.
82, no. 23; London, National
Gallery, 1995, p. 160, no. 58;
Jordan, 1997, pp. 131-6, no.17
B; Cherry and Luna, 2004,
p. 213, no. 30.

Exhibitions
London, National Gallery,
1986-87, no. 27; London,
National Gallery, 1989,
no. 23; London, National
Gallery, 1995, no. 58; Jordan,
1997, no.17 B; Madrid, 2004,
no. 30.

This remarkable still life was painted for an unknown client at the same time as Meléndez was painting his series for the Prince of Asturias. Indeed, the group of oranges here derives from one of his small works of a vertical format from this series, *Still Life with Oranges, Honey Pot, Boxes of Sweetmeats and Watermelon* (cat. 6), with some alterations to accomodate it to the new context. The other elements on the right-hand side of the elaborate composition may have been painted from the life. Once again, this procedure shows that Meléndez's still life arrangements were not always actually in front of the artist as they appear in the final paintings, especially in large-scale compositions such as this one. It also shows how Meléndez used his paintings for the royal series as models for works for private clients, as is suggested by the autograph variants in this exhibition (cats 38, 40).

It was unusual for Meléndez to sign and date his paintings outside the royal series. Here, as in other pictures, the artist's signature is written as if scorched into the wood of a box of sweets and thrust towards the viewer, albeit modestly veiled in shadow. This may reflect Meléndez's particular pride in his performance in this work. Most viewers would concur with this, since the still life is one of his most accomplished works and is carefully orchestrated in formal and chromatic terms. The interplay of rounded

wooden and ceramic containers, and the oblong sweetmeat boxes provides aesthetic pleasure on an almost abstract level. The forms are modelled with emphatic plasticity and a marked monumentality, and they are located in an apparently coherent pictorial space through being drawn in consistent perspective. The chromatic harmony is also carefully controlled and limited to a range of earth hues in the walnuts, wood and terracotta, and the muted orange hue of the fruit. Probably for this reason, Meléndez substituted his original motif of a plate of red azaroles for the present walnuts, as can be seen with x-radiograph photography, while respecting in this conversion the position of the three loose nuts to the left of the plate. The single orange separated from the main group at the far right constitutes a luminous colour accent necessary for the chromatic balance of the composition.

For this still life, Meléndez reused an old canvas, on which a finished bust-length portrait of King Charles III can be seen in x-radiograph photography. Meléndez turned the canvas upside down and overpainted this with his still life. It is reasonable to assume that the portrait was painted by Meléndez some years earlier and its rediscovery is a poignant reminder of the artist's frustrated aspirations as a royal painter and his dramatic career change. **P.C.**

35. Still Life with Fruit, Bread, Cheese and Wine

Oil on canvas, 98 x 133 cm.
Signed on central basket:
L.ˢ M.ᶻ
Madrid, Varez Fisa
collection

Provenance
Sotheby's, New York, 7 June,
1984, lot 125; Private
collection, Geneva (from
which acquired by the
present owner).

Bibliography
Raleigh-Dallas-New York,
1985, p. 122, no. 35; Pérez
Sánchez, 1987, p. 192;
Cherry and Luna, 2004,
p. 216, no. 31.

Exhibitions
Raleigh-Dallas-New York,
1985, no. 35; Seville-
Madrid-Oviedo, 1996-1997,
no. 63; Madrid, 2004, no. 31.

In this still life, Meléndez employed a familiar repertoire of objects to novel effect. The central motif of a basket filled with fruit is a feature of other pictures by the artist, some of which are exhibited here (cats 4, 5). The basket with a white cloth, wine bottle and wine cooler to the right of the composition are elements that also appear in *Still Life with Pears, Wine and Basket* (cat. 33), although these are placed in a freize like arrangement in the latter work, rather than an overlapping arrangement in depth, as here. The wine cooler may well be the same one Meléndez painted in *Still Life with Figs, Bread and Wine* (cat. 3). The motif of the ceramic bowl with metal lid and wooden spoon also appears in *Still Life with Small Pears, Bread, Earthenware Bowl and Glass Bottle* (cat. 1). A more unusual motif here is the plate of cheese. The compositional order of this painting is also consistent with Meléndez's other still lifes, in which large forms close off the composition in the farthest plane and smaller ones occupy the foreground.

However, this painting is unusual in a number of ways. It is one of the largest known still lifes by Meléndez, approaching in scale his monumental *Still Life with Fruit, Bread and Basket in a Landscape* (fig. 66). Moreover, Meléndez has stepped back further from his subject matter than was habitual in

Fig. 66: Luis Meléndez,
Still Life with Fruit, Bread and Basket in a Landscape, c.1772
Oil on canvas, 105,4 x 153,7 cm
New York, The Metropolitan Museum of Art

his paintings. While the other pictures in this exhibition represent the objects from close quarters, the greater distance between the viewer and the subject is evident from the fact that the leg and the corner of the table can be seen, and the greater amount of ambient space around the arrangement. The chromatic composition of an austere palette of earth tones, in which fruit provides the only touches of colour, is reminiscent of other works from Meléndez's later career (cats 33, 34). The painting was probably made for an important client, whose identity remains unknown, and would have constituted an imposing presence in their collection. **P.C.**

36. Still Life with Salmon, Lemon and Kitchen Utensils

Oil on canvas: 41.2 x 62.2 cm
Signed on the edge of
the table:L.S.MZ.DO.ISto.
P.AÑO 1772
Madrid: Prado Museum,
no. 902

Provenance
Royal Collections, Casita
del Príncipe, El Escorial;
Royal Palace of Aranjuez.

Bibliography
Soria, 1948, p. 216; Sánchez
Cantón, 1962, p. 256;
Pothiades, 1963, fig. 135;
Sánchez de Palacios, 1965,
p. 32; Sánchez Cantón, 1966,
p. 256; Newsweek, 1968, p. 99;
Tufts, 1971, p. 164; Torres
Martín, 1971, rep. 6; Buendía,
1973, p. 248; Aparicio, 1973,
p. 26; Pérez Sánchez, 1974,
p. 99; Gaya Nuño, 1977, p. 156;
Bergström, 1977, p. 156;
Lafuente Ferrari, 1978, p. 304;
Luna, 1982-1983, p. 125,
no. 40; Tufts, 1982, no. 1;
Gutiérrez Alonso, 1983,
p. 166; Tufts, 1985a, pp. 83-84;
Blanco Altozano, 1987, p. 121;
Espinosa Martín, 1989b,
p. 72; Rodríguez Gutiérrez de
Ceballos, 1992, p. 203; Morales
y Marín, 1994, p. 220; Luna,
1995, p. 168; Cherry and
Luna, 2004, p. 226, no. 36;
Garrido and Cherry, 2004
[in print], no. 902.

Exhibitions
Tokyo-Kyoto, 1970, no. 93;
Bordeaux, 1978, no. 120;
Madrid-Barcelona, 1982-
1983, no. 40; Valencia, 1984,
no. 31; Raleigh-Dallas-New
York, 1985, no. 27; Paris, 1987-
1988, no. 86; Geneva, 1989,
no. 54; London, 1989, no. 16;
Madrid, 1995, no. 26; Madrid,
2004, no. 36.

This picture, from the artist's period of late maturity, is a magnificent example of his painterly and tactile virtuosity; all of the elements on the canvas are realised with an effective verisimilitude, in which every nuance is captured in a fitting and immediate way. In the foreground, a solitary lemon, on one side, is balanced on the other by kitchen utensils and a splendidly delineated section of salmon. The utensils consist of a copper pot, a copper saucepan and a stewing-pot of Alcorcón manufacture, on top of which is placed a fragment of decorated crockery: this serves as a makeshift lid. Behind this, the handle of what appears to be a wooden spoon is discernible, and at the farthest distance from the viewer's gaze, a spoon with a very long handle completes the composition.

The objects in the picture exude an enormous sense of force and vibrancy which confer a peculiar individuality on each one of them; this is achieved partly by the painterly aplomb with which the objects are rendered as well as the neatness and precision with which shapes and volumes are convincingly represented. Meléndez has constructed here a tableau in which each component plays its own part in a clear and unostentatious way; one is left with the impression that moving objects have, for a moment, become motionless, as if time itself had suddenly stood still: a sort of suspended animation pervades the work. The technique is faultless; one need only emphasise the powerful light effects which produce the sheen on the metal; this effect is rendered by the combination of red and yellow strokes, and the application of a thick *impasto* at certain points, rendered with meticulous exactitude. **J.J.L.**

37. Still Life with Bream, Oranges, Condiments and Kitchen Utensils

Oil on canvas: 42 x 62.2 cm
Signed under the white
cloth in the picture:
L.ˢ.Mᶻ.Dᵒ.1772
Madrid: Prado Museum,
no. 903

Provenance

Royal Collections, Casita
del Príncipe, El Escorial;
Palacio Real de Aranjuez.

Bibliography

Lafuente Ferrari, 1935,
p. 169; Soria, 1948, p. 216;
Lastic, 1955, pp. 44-45;
Lastic, 1955, no. 9, p. 23;
Sánchez Cantón, 1965,
fig. 211; McGraw-Hill, 1970,
fig. 255; Tufts, 1971, p. 165;
Bergström, 1977, p. 157;
Luna, 1982-1983, p. 126,
no. 41; Tufts, 1982, no. 2;
Gutiérrez Alonso, 1983,
p. 166; Pérez Sánchez, 1983-
1984, p. 166, no. 149; Tufts,
1985a, p. 83; Luna, 1995,
p. 166; Cherry and Luna,
2004, p. 230, no. 38; Garrido
and Cherry, 2004 [in print],
no. 903.

Exhibitions

London, 1972, no. 190;
Madrid-Barcelona, 1982-
1983, no. 41; Madrid, 1983-
1984, no. 149; Valencia, 1984,
no. 32; Raleigh-Dallas-New
York, 1985, no. 26; Madrid,
1989-1990, no. 23; Tokyo-
Nagoya, 1992, no. 55;
London, 1995, no. 57;
Jackson, 2001, p. 76;
Madrid, 2004, no. 38.

Two splendidly coloured and finely delineated red bream occupy pride of place in the composition; as a consequence, all other elements are subordinate, in dimension and in position. These objects include oranges, a bulb of garlic, a packet which appears to contain spice, two Alcorcón earthenware bowls, a frying pan with a large handle, a mortar whose handle projects downwards, and an olive-oil bottle which, like the other objects, reflects light in a studied and diversified way. This play of light, with its subtly chromatic tonalities, graphically defines the shapes and dimensions of the objects in the picture, sharply individualising them.

The artist clearly displays here his predilection for the construction of geometric forms; his propensity to reveal the inner design of each object, allocating an individual dimension to each one, is also made manifest. Thus, there is a spatial interplay of cones and inverted cones which, in the background, impart a satisfying finishing touch to the composition. The structural impulse is achieved with a surprising agility, enlivening the whole composition, from the olive-oil bottle to the bream. The fish rise in the centre almost like a monolithic vertical structure; in contrast, the strong horizontal line emphasised by the frying pan, in its linear structure, displays an attempt at the reconciliation of opposing geometrical elements. The coherence of these contrasted geometric stimuli conveys to the eye a balanced reticulated structure of horizontals and verticals which is both supremely aesthetically satisfying and redolent of a muted serenity which pervades the overall composition.

Both the fish and several of the other objects portrayed together are also featured in another work on display in this exhibition (cat. 38). Also, X-ray photographs have indicated the presence (in the area to the left of the kitchen cloth, beside the garlic and behind the bowl) of a shape which, judging by its outlines, was probably intended to represent an onion. J.J.L.

38. Still Life with Bream and Oranges

Oil on canvas, 41 x 62.8 cms.
Signed: L.S E.O M.Z D R.^
D.ZO I S.TO P.E / ANO 1772.
Masaveu collection

Provenance

Bonhams, London,
8 December, 1992, lot 108
(when acquired by the
present owner).

Bibliography

Luna, 1995, no. 57; London,
1995, p. 159, no. 57; Cherry
and Luna, 2004, p. 231,
no. 39.

Exhibitions

London, 1995, no. 57;
Seville-Madrid-Oviedo,
1996-1997, no. 65;
Madrid, 2004, no. 39.

This painting is a close variant of the *Still Life with Bream, Oranges, Condiments and Kitchen Utensils* from the royal collection (cat. 37). The main motifs of the composition — the bream propped up against an overturned bowl, tin funnel, oranges and kitchen cloth — have been transferred from the primary version. These elements are not, however, copied exactly by the artist. In the new version, the fish have been moved to the left of centre, with a greater distance between these and the oranges, the right hand one of which is represented whole. There are consequent differences in the fold configuration of the kitchen cloth, the rind and leaves of the oranges, and in details of the bream, such as the diamond pattern of scales on the body of the uppermost fish. Both pictures represent garlic bulbs, a packet of spices and a small ceramic bowl occupying similar locations in the composition, although these are represented differently in each work. In this version, Meléndez has altered the composition with additional elements; a ceramic vinegar bottle and a beaten bronze cauldron that marks an emphatic diagonal compositional accent.

Meléndez evidently considered the still life he painted for the Prince of Asturias (cat. 37) a consummate composition, that was worth repeating. This variation was painted in the same year as the royal picture, probably while it was still in his studio. The painting is unique among Meléndez's known variants in being signed and dated. This suggests that the paintings had an equivalent status for Meléndez as two "originals", rather than merely a primary and a secondary version of a composition. The picture is certainly on a par with the Prado still life in terms of its quality of execution. There is no perceptible abbreviation of technique vis-a-vis its supposed prototype, as occurs in some of Meléndez's other variants and both paintings are distinguished by their rich, painterly handling and fine detail. **P.C.**

39. *Still Life with Partridges, Onions, Cloves of Garlic and Kitchen Utensils*

Oil on canvas: 41.6 x 62.3 cm
Signed on the edge of the
table: L^S.M^Z.
Madrid: Prado Museum,
no. 908

Provenance
Royal Collections, Casita
del Príncipe, El Escorial;
Palacio Real de Aranjuez.

Bibliography
Mayer, 1942, p. 512; Serullaz,
1947, p. 478; Soria, 1948,
p. 216; Lafuente Ferrari,
1953, fig. 255; Chueca
Goitia, 1958, fig. 164; Tufts,
1971, p. 166; Luna, 1982-
1983, p. 128, no.42; Tufts,
1982, no. 7; Gutiérrez
Alonso, 1983, p. 166; Luna,
1984, p. 156; Tufts, 1985a,
pp. 82-83; Luna, 1995,
p. 164; Cherry and Luna,
2004, p.. 218, no. 32; Garrido
and Cherry, 2004 [in print],
no. 908.

Exhibitions
Madrid-Barcelona, 1982-
1983, no. 42; Valencia, 1984,
no. 33; Florence, 1986, no.
76; Madrid, 2004, no. 32.

Although hunting scenes are rarely encountered in the *oeuvre* of Meléndez, dead birds sometimes appear in his canvases; here, two partridges, with variegated plumage, lie prone in the foreground. They form the principal point of interest in the composition, as is also the case in another work in this exhibition (cat. 40).

The other motifs which fill the space in the foreground of the picture include the bulbs and cloves of garlic, the paper parcels, and onions scattered about. Behind these, two large earthenware bowls – manufactured at the Alcorcón factory, near Madrid – occupy much of the middle ground: one of these is turned over on its side while the other, more securely positioned on the table, contains three china dishes, each of them decorated with floral motifs of the type known as *adormidera* (opium poppy); this feature most likely points to Talavera (i.e. Talavera de la Reina, near Toledo) or Puente del Arzobispo as the place of manufacture. Most of the objects in the foreground are shown propped up against the bowls at the back, conferring a principle of unity on the entire scene, which appears overall to be a graphic illustration of a busy kitchen where cooking is about to take place.

Even with a perfunctory examination of the composition of the picture's contents, one can quickly appreciate a habitual tendency of the artist: his practice of juxtaposing objects and substances which differ in shape, size and consistency; thus, large objects are often positioned in close relationship with smaller elements, and rough surfaces intermingle with smooth. Larger objects of a bulky construction (especially table utensils and vessels) assume an imposing, architectonic grandeur which is truly impressive; this sense of hardness, almost of an intimidating nature, is conveyed here in the realistic depiction of the objects' surfaces. **J.J.L.**

40. *Still Life with Partridges*

Oil on canvas, 42 x 62 cm.
Signed on table at lower
right: L. M.ᵈ D.ᵒ ANO 1773.
Masaveu collection

Provenance
Edmund Peel and Asociates
Sale, Madrid, 29 October,
1991, lot 5 (when acquired
by the present owner).

Bibliography
Cherry and Luna, 2004,
p. 219, no. 30.

Exhibitions
Madrid, 2004, no. 30.

The brace of partridge propped up against an overturned bowl and three onions repeat these motifs, with only the slightest of differences, in the undated *Still Life with Partridges, Onions, Cloves of Garlic and Kitchen Utensils* from the royal collection of the same format and of approximately the same size (cat. 39). Meléndez may have used a tracing to transfer the motifs from one picture to the other and locate them in a similar position on the tabletop, while the prototype was still in the artist's possession. While the present painting is signed and dated 1773, it is unclear which picture preceded the other. A close examination of the partridge and onions in both paintings shows that these elements in the present picture are painted in a slightly less meticulous manner than those in the work from the royal collection, that is perhaps to be expected when an artist copies his own work. However, the smaller upturned bowl in the present version in fact repeats the original sized bowl of the royal picture, that Meléndez repainted and extended towards the right.

The main motifs are accompanied by objects that the artist is likely to have observed from nature. A single packet of spices occupies a similar location to the two spice packets in the royal picture, placed to one side of the table, as in many other of Meléndez's still lifes. Behind this is a mortar and pestle, and a kitchen cloth. The left-hand side of the composition is occupied by a large jug of Alcorcón ware with its opening sealed by a shard of Talavera pottery, whose well-worn edges show that this has been long used for this purpose in the kitchen.

This exhibition provides an opportunity to compare closely related compositions, that were never intended to be seen together once they left the artist's studio. It is unlikely that the close formal relationships between the still lifes with partridge shown here would have been recognised by collectors in Meléndez's lifetime, given the presence of one of the works in the private collection of the Prince of Asturias. Judging the pictures independently and on their own merits, however, all of the component elements share the same high degree of verismilitude and convincingly appear to have been painted from actual arrangements set up before the artist. **P.C.**

Bibliography

Águeda Villar, 1981
M. Águeda Villar, "Mengs y la Academia de Bellas Artes de San Fernando", in M. Águeda Villar, *ii Symposium sobre Feijóo*, Oviedo, 1981.

Águeda Villar, 1982
M. Águeda Villar, "La colección de pinturas del Infante Don Sebastián Gabriel de Borbón", in *Boletín del Museo del Prado*, 8, 1982, pp. 102-117.

Aguilera, 1946
E. M. Aguilera, *Pintores españoles del siglo xviii*, Barcelona, 1946.

Agulló y Cobo, 1978
M. Agulló y Cobo, *Noticias sobre Pintores Madrileños de los siglos xvi y xvii*, Granada-Madrid, 1978.

Agulló y Cobo, 1981
M. Agulló y Cobo, *Más noticias sobre Pintores Madrileños de los siglos xvi al xviii*, Madrid, 1981.

Agulló y Cobo, 1994
M. Agulló y Cobo, *Documentos para la Historia de la pintura española*, Madrid, 1994.

Ainaud de Lasarte, 1952
J. Ainaud de Lasarte, *Cerámica y vidrio*, Ars Hispaniae x, Madrid, 1952.

Albert de León, 1998
M. Á. Albert de León, "Una colección de cerámica colonial mexicana", in *Boletín del Museo*, Museo del Virreinato, Tepotzotlán, November 1998, no. 16, p. 9.

Alcahali, 1897
Barón de Alcahali, *Diccionario biográfico de artistas valencianos*, Valencia, 1897.

Alcolea, 1959-1962
S. Alcolea, "La pintura en Barcelona durante el siglo xviii", in *Anales y Boletín de los Museos de Arte de Barcelona*, xiv and xv, Barcelona, 1959-1960 and 1961-1962.

Alcolea, 1967
S. Alcolea, "Mariano Salvador Maella". *The Register of the Museum of Art*. Kansas, iii, Winter, 1967, p. 24.

Aldana Fernández, 1968
S. Aldana Fernández, "Benito Espinós, pintor académico", in *Archivo de Arte Valenciano*, vol. 1, Valencia, 1968.

Aldana Fernández, 1970
S. Aldana Fernández, *Pintores Valencianos de Flores (1766-1866)*, Valencia, 1970.

Alomar, 1975
G. Alomar, "En el tercer centenario de Guillermo Mesquida", in *Diario de Mallorca*, Palma de Mallorca, 9th April 1975.

Altamiras, 1994
J. Altamiras, *Nuevo arte de la cocina*, Zaragoza, 1994.

Amador de los Ríos y Rada y Delgado, 1983
J. Amador de los Ríos y J. D. Rada y Delgado, *Historia de la Villa y Corte de Madrid*, Madrid, 1983.

Andiol, 1976
R. Andiol, *Teatro y sociedad en el Madrid del siglo xviii*, Madrid, 1976.

Anes, 1969
G. Anes, *Economía e Ilustración en la España del siglo xviii*, Madrid, 1969.

Anes, 1975
G. Anes, *El Antiguo Régimen. Los Borbones*, Madrid, 1975.

Angulo Íñiguez, 1971
D. Angulo Iñiguez, *Pintura del siglo xvii*, Ars Hispaniae, vol. xv, Madrid, 1971.

Angulo Íñiguez, 1975
D. Angulo Iñiguez, *Murillo y su escuela*, Seville, 1975.

Angulo Íñiguez, 1980
D. Angulo Iñiguez, *Murillo*, 3 vols., Madrid, 1980.

Aparicio Olmos, 1966
E. M. Aparicio Olmos, *Palomino: su arte y su tiempo*, Valencia, 1966.

Aparicio, 1973
O. Aparicio, *Los bodegones en la pintura del Museo del Prado*, Madrid, 1973.

Apollonio, 1960
V. Apollonio, *La natura morta nella pintura italiana*, Milan, 1960.

Arisi, 1986
F. Arisi, *Gian Paolo Panini e i fasti della Roma del '700*, Roma, 1986.

Armstrong, 1892
E. Armstrong, *Elisabeth Farnèse*, London, 1892.

Arrese, 1973
J. L. Arrese, *Antonio González Ruiz*, Madrid, 1973.

Avilés Fernández, 1973
M. Avilés Fernández, *La instauración borbónica*, Madrid, 1973.

Ayres de Carvalho, 1960-1962
A. Ayres de Carvalho, *Don João V e a Arte do seu tempo*, Lisbon, 1960-1962.

Azcárate Luxán, 1987
I. Azcárate Luxán, "Cristóbal Vilella: un naturalista en la Academia", in *Academia*, no. 64, 1987, pp. 419-432.

Azcárate Luxán, 1990
I. Azcárate Luxán, *Naturaleza y arte. La fauna de la Isla de Mallorca in la obra de Cristóbal Vilella*, Patrimonio Nacional y José J. de Olañeta, Palma de Mallorca, 1990.

Barrenechea, 1956
M. T. Barrenechea, *María Bárbara de Braganza*, Madrid, 1956.

Bartolomé, 1999
A. Bartolomé (ed.), *Las artes decorativas en España*, Summa Artis, xlv, Madrid, 1999.

Battersby, 1974
M. Battersby, *Trompe l'oeil. The Eye Deceived*, London, 1974.

Baticle, 1966
J. Baticle, «Les attachés françaises de Luis Paret y Alcázar», in *Revue du Louvre*, no. 3, 1966.

Baudrillart, 1890
A. Baudrillart, *Philippe V et la Cour de France*, Paris, 1890.

Bayón, 1970
D. Bayón, «Originalidad y significado de las primeras naturalezas muertas españolas», in *R.I.E.*, 109, 1970, pp. 3-41.

Bazin, 1960
G. Bazin, *A Gallery of Flowers*, London, 1960.

Bazin, 1964
G. Bazin, *Baroque and Rococo*, London, 1964.

Bazin, 1967
G. Bazin, *Le temps des Musées*,
Liege-Brussels, 1967.

Bédat, 1974
C. Bédat, *L'Académie des Beaux-Arts de Madrid* (1744-1808),
Toulouse, 1974.

Bédat, 1989
C. Bédat, La *Real Academia de
Bellas Artes de San Fernando*,
(1744-1808), Madrid, 1989

Beltrán Martínez, 1964
A. Beltrán Martínez, *Catálogo del
Museo Provincial de Bellas Artes de
Zaragoza*, Zaragoza, 1964.

Benedito y Vives, 1926
M. Benedito y Vives, *La Real
Fábrica de Tapices de Madrid*,
Madrid, 1926.

Benet, 1947
R. Benet, *Viladomat*, Barcelona,
1947.

Bénezit, 1999
E. Bénezit, *Dictionnaire des peintres,
sculpteurs, dessinateurs et graveurs*,
Gründ, 1999.

Bergström, 1956
I. Bergström, *Dutch Still Life
Painting in the Seventeenth Century*,
London-New York, 1956.

Bergström, 1970
I. Bergström, *Maestros españoles de
Bodegones y Floreros del siglo xvii*,
Madrid, 1970.

Bergström, 1977
I. Bergström, «Preistoria di un
genere», in *Natura in posa*, Milan,
1977.

Bergström, 1979
I. Bergström et al., *Stilleben*, Zurich,
1979.

Biederman, 1993
A. Biederman, *Diccionario de
símbolos*, Barcelona, 1993.

Blanco Altozano, 1987
P. Blanco Altozano, "Luis Meléndez:
análisis estético y significativo de sus
bodegones", in *Congreso Nacional
El Arte de las Cortes Europeas del
siglo xviii*, Madrid-Aranjuez, 1987,
pp. 121-128.

Blunt, 1967
A. Blunt, "Don Vincenzo Vittoria",
in *The Burlington Magazine*, CIX,
January, 1967.

Bocchi and Spike, 1992
G. and U. Bocchi and J. T. Spike,
*Naturalia. Nature morte in collezioni
pubbliche e private*, Turin, 1992.

Bottineau, 1986
Y. Bottineau, *L'Art de Cour dans
l'Espagne des Lumières. 1746-1808*,
Paris, 1986.

Bottineau, 1993a
Y. Bottineau, *L'art de cour dans
l'Espagne de Philippe V, 1700-1746*,
[Bordeaux, 1962] Paris, 1993.

Bottineau, 1993b
Y. Bottineau, *Les Bourbons
d'Espagne*, Paris, 1993.

Brown, 1978
J. Brown, *Images and Ideas in
Seventeenth Century Spanish
Painting*, Princeton, 1978
[Madrid, 1980].

Brown, 1981
J. Brown, *The Golden Age of
Painting in Spain*, New Haven-London, 1981 [Madrid, 1990].

Bru Romo, 1971
M. Bru Romo, *La Academia
Española de Bellas Artes en Roma*,
Madrid, 1971.

Brunetti, Causa, Faldi, 1964
E. Brunetti, R. Causa, I. Faldi *et al.*,
La natura morta italiana, Milan,
1964.

Bryson, 1990
N. Bryson, *Looking at the
Overlooked. Four Essays on Still Life
Painting*, London, 1990.

Buendía, 1973
J. R. Buendía, *El Prado básico*,
Madrid, 1973.

Bye, 1921
A. E. Bye, *Pots and pans*, Princeton,
1921.

Calatayud, 1987
M. A. Calatayud, *Real Gabinete de
Historia Natural 1752-1786*, Madrid,
1987.

Calvo Serraller, 1981
F. Calvo Serraller, *Teoría de la
pintura del Siglo de Oro*, Madrid,
1981.

Calvo Serraller, 1999
F. Calvo Serraller, *El bodegón
español [de Zurbarán a Picasso]*,
Museo de Bellas Artes de Bilbao,
1999.

Camón Aznar, 1977
Camón Aznar, *La pintura española
del siglo xvii*, Summa Artis, xxv,
Madrid, 1977.

**Camón Aznar, Morales and Valdivieso,
1984**
J. Camón Aznar, J. L. Morales y
Marín and E. Valdivieso, *Arte
español del siglo xviii*, Summa Artis,
xxvii, Madrid, 1984.

Camps Cazorla, 1936
E. Camps Cazorla, *Cerámica
española*, Madrid, 1936.

Carrera y Pujal, 1951
J. Carrera y Pujal, *La Barcelona del
siglo xviii*, Barcelona, 1951.

Carrete Parrondo, 1989
J. Carrete Parrondo et al., *El grabado
en España. Siglo xv al xviii*, Summa
Artis, xxxi, Madrid, 1989.

Casanovas, 1981
M. A. Casanovas, "Alcora", in
Cerámica esmaltada española,
Barcelona, 1981.

Casanovas, 1989
M. A. Casanovas, "Cerámica de
Alcora", *Colección del Banco
Hispanoamericano*, Madrid, 1989.

Cassou, 1952
J. Cassou, "La nature morte
espagnole", in *Verve*, no. 26-28,
1952.

Causa, 1961
R. Causa, *Pittura Napoletana dal xv
al xix Secolo*, Bergamo, 1961.

Causa, 1972
R. Causa, *Natura morta a Napoli nel
Seicento-Settecento*, Storia di Napoli,
vol. v, Naples, 1972.

Caveda, 1867
J. Caveda, *Memorial para la historia
de la Real Academia de San
Fernando*, Madrid, 1867.

Cavestany, 1922
J. Cavestany, "Pintores españoles
de flores", in *Arte Español*, 6, 1922,
p. 124.

Cavestany, 1936-1940
J. Cavestany, *Floreros y bodegones en la pintura española*, Sociedad Española de Amigos del Arte, Madrid, 1936-1940.

Ceán Bermúdez, 1965
J. A. Ceán Bermúdez, *Diccionario de los más ilustres profesores de las bellas artes en España*, 6 vols. [Madrid, 1800] ed. facsimile, Madrid, 1965.

Chastenet, 1966
J. Chastenet, *La vie quotidienne en Espagne au temps de Goya*, Paris, 1966.

Cherry, 1984
P. Cherry, exhibition review "Pintura española de bodegones y floreros de 1600 a Goya", in *The Burlington Magazine*, cxxvi, 1984, p. 60.

Cherry, 1995
P. Cherry, *Tres siglos de pintura*, Caylus Anticuario, Madrid, 1995.

Cherry, 1997
P. Cherry, *Pinturas de cuatro siglos*, Caylus Anticuario, Madrid, 1997.

Cherry, 1999
P. Cherry, "Arte y naturaleza", in *El bodegón español en el Siglo de Oro*, Madrid, 1999.

Cherry, 2004 [forthcoming]
P. Cherry, *Luis Meléndez. Still Life Painter*, 2004 [forthcoming].

Cherry and Luna, 2004
Peter Cherry and Juan L. Luna, *Luis Meléndez. Bodegones*, exh. cat., Museo Nacional del Prado, Madrid, 2004.

Chueca Goitia, 1958
F. Chueca Goitia, *Madrid y Sitios Reales*, Barcelona, 1958.

Chueca Goitia, 1971
F. Chueca Goitia, *Invariantes castizos de la arquitectura española*, Madrid, 1971.

Cian, 1896
V. Cian, *Italia e Spagna del secolo xviii*, Turin, 1896.

Corral, 2000
J. del Corral, *La vida cotidiana en el Madrid del siglo xviii*, Madrid, 2000.

Cottino, 2000
A. Cottino, "Novità sull'attività giovanile di Luis Meléndez", in *L'arte nella storia. Contributi di critica e storia dell'arte per Gianni Carlo Sciolla*, V. Terraroli, F. Varallo and L. de Fanti, eds., 2000, pp. 165-170,

Cottino, 2003
A. Cottino, *La natura morta italiana dal Caravaggio al Settecento*, Palazzo Strozzi, Florence, 2003.

Danvila, 1905
A. Danvila, *Fernando VI y Bárbara de Braganza*, Madrid, 1905.

Delgado, 1957
O. Delgado, *Paret y Alcázar*, Madrid, 1957.

Desdevizes du Dezert, 1897-1904
G. N. Desdevizes du Dezert, *L'Espagne de l'ancien régime*, Paris, 1897-1904.

Díaz Padrón, 1975
M. Díaz Padrón, *Museo del Prado. Catálogo de pinturas. I Pintura flamenca, siglo xvii*, Madrid, 1975.

Diccionario de Autoridades, 1984
Diccionario de Autoridades, t. ii, ed. of 1726 facsimile, ed. Gredos, Madrid, 1984.

Domínguez Ortiz, 1976
A. Domínguez Ortiz, *Sociedad y Estado en el siglo xviii español*, Barcelona, 1976.

Dominici, 1742-1745
B. de Dominici, *Vite de' pittori, scultori ed architetti napoletani*, 3 vols., Naples, 1742-1745.

Duby, 1991
G. Duby (ed.), *Historia de la vida privada*, Madrid, 1991.

Duplá del Moral, 1990
A. Duplá del Moral (ed.), *Madrid in el Archivo Histórico de Protocolos*, Madrid, 1990.

Duque Oliart, 1986
M. Duque Oliart, "Pintura de flores: la obra de Juan de Arellano", in *Goya*, 191, 1986, pp. 272-279.

El bodegón, 2000
El bodegón, collaboration by Berger, Calvo Serraller, Castilla del Pino, Checa, Cherry, De Antonio, Finaldi, Jarauta, Pérez Sánchez, Sánchez Vidal, Sarabia, Schneider, Segal, Seseña, Stoichita, Tapié, Tongiorgi Tomasi, Riadó y Vischer, Fundación Amigos del Museo del Prado, Madrid, 2000.

Enciclopedia, n.d.
Enciclopedia General Ilustrada, vol. xxxiv, Espasa Calpe, n.d., Madrid.

Espinosa Martín, 1989a
M. C. Espinosa Martín, "El retrato miniatura de los regalos diplomáticos españoles en el siglo xviii", in *El Arte en las cortes europeas del siglo xviii*. Comunicaciones de Congreso en Aranjuez, 27-29th April 1987, Dirección General de Patrimonio Cultural, Madrid, 1989, pp. 264-268.

Espinosa Martín, 1989b
M. C. Espinosa Martín, "Aportes documentales a los bodegones de Luis Meléndez", in *Boletín del Museo del Prado*, x, 1989, pp. 67-77.

Espinosa Martín, 2000
M. C. Espinosa Martín, in *El documento pintado: cinco siglos de arte en manuscritos*, exh. cat., Museo Nacional del Prado, Madrid, 2000.

European Masters, 1954-1955
European Masters of the Eighteenth Century, Royal Academy of Arts, London, 1954-1955.

Faré, 1962
M. Faré, *La nature morte en France*, Paris, 1962.

Faré, 1974
M. Faré, *Le grand siècle de la nature morte en France, le xviie siècle*, Freiburg, 1974.

Faré, 1975
M. Faré, "De quelques termes designant la peinture d'objets", in *Études d'Art…Sterling*, Paris, 1975.

Faré, 1976
M. y F. Faré, *La vie silencieuse en France. La nature morte au xviie siècle*, Freiburg, 1976.

Ferrari y Scavizzi, 1992
O. Ferrari y G. Scavizzi, *Luca Giordano*, Naples, [1966] 1992.

Ferrer del Río, 1856
A. Ferrer del Río, *Historia del reinado de Carlos III en España*, Madrid, 1856.

Fontaine, 1909
A. Fontaine, *Les doctrines d'art en France*, Paris, 1909.

Fontaine, 1914
A. Fontaine, *Academiciens d'autrefois*, Paris, 1914.

Fontbona and Durá, 1999
F. Fontbona andand V. Durá, *Cataleg del Museu de la Reial Académia des Belles Arts de Sant Jordi I (pintura)*, Barcelona, 1999.

Frothingham, 1963
A. W. Frothingham, *Spanish Glass*, New York, 1963.

Gallego, 1979
A. Gallego, *Historia del grabado en España*, Madrid, 1979.

Gállego, 1972
J. Gállego, *Visión y símbolos de la pintura española del Siglo de Oro*, Madrid, 1972.

Gállego, 1976
J. Gállego, *El pintor de artesano a artista*, Granada, 1976.

Garín y Ortiz de Taranco, 1945
F. M. Garín y Ortiz de Taranco, *La Academia Valenciana de Bellas Artes*, Valencia, 1945.

Garrido and Cherry, 2004 [forthcoming]
C. Garrido and P. Cherry, *Luis Meléndez: la serie de bodegones para el Príncipe de Asturias. Estudio técnico*, Madrid, 2004.

Gasser, 1961
M. Gasser, *Das Selbstbildnis*, Zurich, 1961.

Gassier y Wilson, 1974
P. Gassier y J. Wilson, *Vida y obra de Francisco de Goya*, Barcelona, 1974.

Gaya Nuño, 1946
J. A. Gaya Nuño, *Historia del arte español*, Madrid, 1946.

Gaya Nuño, 1950a
J. A. Gaya Nuño, *Madrid*, Aries, Barcelona, 1950

Gaya Nuño, 1950b
J. A. Gaya Nuño, *Autorretratos de artistas españoles*, Barcelona, 1950.

Gaya Nuño, 1952
J. A. Gaya Nuño, "Luis Paret y Alcázar", in *Boletín de la Sociedad Española de Excursiones*, 1952.

Gaya Nuño, 1957
J. A. Gaya Nuño, *Palomino*, Córdoba, 1957.

Gaya Nuño, 1970
J. A. Gaya Nuño, "Rococó, neoclasicismo y romanticismo en el arte de España del siglo xviii", in *Cuadernos de la Cátedra Feijóo*, 1970.

Gaya Nuño, 1975
J. A. Gaya Nuño, *Historia de la crítica de arte en España*, Madrid, 1975.

Gestoso Pérez, 1900
J. Gestoso Pérez, *Ensayo de un diccionario de los artífices que florecieron en Sevilla desde el siglo xvii al xviii inclusive*, Seville, 1900.

Gombrich, 1978
E. H. Gombrich, "Tradition and Expression in Western Still Life" [1959], in *Meditations on a Hobby Horse*, London, [1963] 1978, pp. 95-105.

Gómez Moreno, 1951
M. E. Gómez Moreno, *Breve historia de la escultura española*, Madrid, 1951.

Gómez Moreno, 1958
M. E. Gómez Moreno, *Escultura del siglo xvii*, Ars Hispaniae xvi, Madrid, 1958.

Gómez de la Serna, 1982
R. Gómez de la Serna, Prologue to "Pregones de ayer y de hoy" in *Los gritos de Madrid*, facsimile ed. of the collection of 72 engravings of 1798, Madrid, 1982.

Gregori, 2003
M. Gregori, *La natura morta italiana. Da Caravaggio al Settecento*, Florence, 2003.

Greindl, 1983
E. Greindl, *Les peintres flamands de nature morte au xviie siècle*, Brussels [1956], enl. ed. 1983.

Grimm, 1942
C. Grimm, *Natures mortes, flamands, hollandaises et allemandes aux xvii et xviii siècles*, Paris, 1942.

Grimm, 1988
C. Grimm, *Stilleben. Die niederländischen und deutschen Meister*, Stuttgart-Zurich, 1988.

Gudiol, 1941
J. Gudiol, *Spanish Painting*, Toledo, 1941.

Gudiol, 1970
J. Gudiol, *Goya 1746-1828*, Barcelona, 1970.

Gudiol, Alcolea and Cirlot, n.d.
J. Gudiol, S. Alcolea and J. E. Cirlot, *Historia de la pintura en Cataluña*, Madrid, n.d.

Guinard, 1956
P. Guinard, "Complexité de la Peinture Espagnole au xviiie siècle", in *C. B.*, 1956.

Guldener, 1950
H. Guldener, *Flowers: the Flowerpiece in Painting*, 1950.

Gutiérrez Alonso, 1983
L. C. Gutiérrez Alonso, "Precisiones a la cerámica de los bodegones de Luis Egidio Meléndez", in *Boletín del Museo del Prado*, xii, September-December 1983, pp. 162-166.

Gwyne-Jones, 1954
A. Gwyne-Jones, *Introduction to Still Life*, London, 1954.

Haig, 1913
E. Haig, *The Floral Symbolism of the Great Master*, 1913.

Hairs, 1965
M. L. Hairs, *Les peintres flamands de fleurs au 17ème siècle*, [1955], 2nd ed. Paris-Brussels, 1965.

Haraszti-Takacs, 1983
M. Haraszti-Takacs, *Spanish Genre Painting in the Seventeenth Century*, Budapest, 1983.

Held, 1971
J. Held, *Die genrebilder der Madrid Teppichmanufaktur and die Anfänge Goyas*, Berlin, 1971.

Henares Cuéllar, 1977
J. Henares Cuéllar, *La teoría de las artes plásticas en España en la segunda mitad del siglo xviii*, Granada, 1977.

Herr, 1971
R. Herr, *España y la revolución del siglo xviii*, [Princeton, 1969], Madrid, 1971.

Herrero García, 1933
M. Herrero García, "Las bebidas", in *La vida española del siglo xvii*, Madrid, 1933.

Herrero García, 1943
M. Herrero García, *Contribución de la literatura a la Historia del Arte*, Madrid, 1943.

Inventarios Reales, n.d.
Inventarios Reales, Archivo del Palacio de Oriente, (unpublished manuscript), Madrid, n.d.

Inventarios Reales, 1746
Inventarios Reales, La Granja de San Ildefonso, 1746.

Jacquet, 1968
J. L. Jacquet, *Les Bourbons d'Espagne*, Lausanne, 1968.

Jahier, 1996
H. Jahier, "El reloj y la pluma. Un suizo en la España del último año del reinado de Fernando VI", in *Vida cotidiana en tiempos de Goya*, exh. cat. [organised by Natacha Seseña], Museo Arqueológico, Madrid, 1996, p. 63.

Jordan, 1967
W. Jordan, *Juan van der Hamen*, Ann Arbor, 1967.

Jordan, 1997
W. B. Jordan, An Eye on Nature: *Spanish Still Life Paintings from Sánchez Cotán to Goya*, exh. cat. Matthiessen Fine Art Ltd., London, 1997.

Jordan and Cherry, 1995
W. B. Jordan and P. Cherry, *Spanish Still Life from Velázquez to Goya*, exh. cat., London-Madrid, 1995.

Junquera y Mato, 1976
J. J. Junquera y Mato, "En torno a la pintura española de género", in *Revista de Occidente*, July-December, 1976, p. 76.w

Junquera y Mato, 1979
J. J. Junquera y Mato, *La decoración y el mobiliario de los palacios de Carlos IV*, Madrid, 1979.

Junquera de Vega, 1965
P. Junquera de Vega, "Los libros de Coro de la Real Capilla", in *Reales Sitios*, no. 6, 1965, pp. 12-27.

Junquera de Vega, 1973-1974
P. Junquera de Vega, "M. S. Maella", in *Reales Sitios*, no. 37-41, 1973-1974.

Junquera de Vega and Ruiz Alcón, 1958
P. Junquera de Vega and M. T. Ruiz Alcón, *Guía ilustrada del Real Palacio de Aranjuez*, Madrid, 1958.

Kalnein and Levey, 1972
G. Kalnein and M. Levey, *Art and Architecture of the Eighteenth Century in France*, Harmonsdworth, 1972.

Kany, 1932
C. Kany *Life and Manners in Madrid* 1750-1800, Berkeley, 1932.

Kinkead, 1978
D. Kinkead, *Juan de Valdés Leal (1622-1690). His Life and Work*, New York, 1978.

Kubler, 1957
G. Kubler, *Arquitectura de los siglos xvii y xviii*, Ars Hispaniae, xiv, Madrid, 1957.

Kubler and Soria, 1959
G. Kubler and M. Soria, *Art and Architecture in Spain, Portugal and its American Dominions*, London, 1959.

Kuoni, 1981
B. Kuoni, *Cestería tradicional ibérica*, Barcelona, 1981.

Kutznetsov, 1966
J. Kutznetsov, *West-European Still Life Painting*, Moscow, 1966.

Lafuente Ferrari, 1935
E. Lafuente Ferrari, "La Peinture de Bodegones en Espagne", in *Gazette des Beaux-Arts*, xiv, 1935, ii, pp. 169-183.

Lafuente Ferrari, 1944
E. Lafuente Ferrari, "Borrascas de la pintura y triunfo de su excelencia", in *Archivo Español de Arte*, no. 62, March, 1944.

Lafuente Ferrari, 1946
E. Lafuente Ferrari, "Comparación entre el arte francés y el español en el siglo xviii", in *Bulletin de la Bibliothèque de l'Institut Français en Espagne*, junio, 1946, ii, pp. 16-19.

Lafuente Ferrari, 1947
E. Lafuente Ferrari, *Antecedentes, coincidencias e influencias del arte de Goya*, Madrid, 1947.

Lafuente Ferrari, 1953
E. Lafuente Ferrari, *Breve historia de la Pintura Española*, París, 1953.

Lafuente Ferrari, 1978
E. Lafuente Ferrari, *Museo del Prado: La Pintura Española de los siglos xvii y xviii*, Madrid, 1978.

Lambert, 1945
E. Lambert, *L'art en Espagne et au Portugal*, Paris, 1945.

Larruga, 1973
E. Larruga, *Memorias políticas y económicas sobre frutos, fábricas y minas de España*, Madrid, 1973.

Lastic, 1955a
G. de Lastic, "Un portraitiste des biens de la terre", in *L'œil*, no. 9, 1955.

Lastic, 1955b
G. de Lastic, "Rustic Fare for the Spanish Court", in *The Selective Eye*, 1955.

Lauts, 1969
J. Lauts, Stilleben *alter Meister I. Niederländer und Deutsche*, Karlsruhe, 1969.

Lauts, 1970
J. Lauts, *Stilleben alter Meister II. Franzosen*, Karlsruhe, 1970.

Lavalle-Cobo, 2002
T. Lavalle-Cobo, *Isabel de Farnesio la reina coleccionista*, Madrid, 2002.

Lefort, 1983
P. Lefort, *La peinture espagnole*, Paris, 1983.

León Tello and Sanz Sanz, 1979
F. J. León Tello and M. M. V. Sanz Sanz, *La estética académica española en el siglo xviii: Real Academia de Bellas Artes de San Carlos de Valencia*, Valencia, 1979.

Levey, 1987
M. Levey, *The National Gallery Collection*, London, 1987.

Logu, 1962
G. de Logu, *Natura morta italiana*, Bergamo, 1962.

López-Rey, 1948
J. López-Rey, "Goya's Still Lifes", in *Art Quarterly*, xi, 1948.

López-Rey, 1964
J. López-Rey, *Introduction to Spanish Still Life Painting*, Newark, 1964.

Lozoya, 1943
Marqués de Lozoya, *Vicente López (1772-1850)*, Barcelona, 1943.

Luna, 1973a
J. J. Luna, "Obras de Jean Pillement en colecciones españolas", in *Archivo Español de Arte*, no. 184, 1973.

Luna, 1973b
J. J. Luna, "Inventario y almoneda de algunas pinturas de la colección de Isabel de Farnesio", in *Boletín del Seminario de Arte y Arqueología de la Universidad de Valladolid*, 1973.

Luna, 1973c
J. J. Luna, "Jean Ranc, Pintor de Cámara de Felipe V. Aspectos inéditos", in *Actas xxiii Congreso Internacional de Historia del Arte*, iii, Granada, 1973.

Luna, 1974-1976
J. J. Luna, "Michel-Ange Houasse", in *Reales Sitios*, no. 42, 1974, no. 43, 44, 45, 1975, no. 47, 48, 1976.

Luna, 1975
J. J. Luna, "Un centenario olvidado: Jean Ranc", in *Goya*, no. 127, 1975, p. 22.

Luna, 1977
J. J. Luna, "Jean Ranc", in *Reales Sitios*, no. 51, 1977, p. 65.

Luna, 1978a
J. J. Luna, "Louis-Michel van Loo en España", in *Goya*, no. 144, 1978.

Luna, 1978b
J. J. Luna, "Rigaud et l'Espagne", in *Gazette des Beaux-Arts*, May-June, 1978, p. 185.

Luna, 1979a [unpublished]
J. J. Luna, *La pintura francesa de los siglos xvii y xviii en España*, doctoral thesis, Universidad Complutense, Madrid, 1979 [unpublished].

Luna, 1979b
J. J. Luna, "El retrato de Fernando VI y Bárbara de Braganza con su Corte por Amigoni", in *Archivo Español de Arte*, no. 207, 1979.

Luna, 1980a
J. J. Luna, "Mengs en la Corte de Madrid. Notas y documentos", in *Anales del Instituto de Estudios Madrileños*, 1980.

Luna, 1980b
J. J. Luna, "Jean Ranc. Ideas artísticas y métodos de trabajo a través de pinturas y documentos", in *Archivo Español de Arte*, 1980, p. 449.

Luna, 1981a
J. J. Luna, "Houasse en la Corte de Madrid. Notas y documentos", in *Anales del Instituto de Estudios Madrileños*, 1981.

Luna, 1981b
J. J. Luna, "Introducción al estudio de Charles-Joseph Flipart en España", in *Libro Homenaje a don Antonio Domínguez Ortiz*, Madrid, 1981.

Luna, 1981c
J. J. Luna, "Presencia de Jean Pillement en la España del siglo xviii", in *i Jornadas de Arte*, C. S. I. C., Madrid, 1981.

Luna, 1981-1982
J. J. Luna, *Michel-Ange Houasse, pintor de la corte de Felipe V*, Museo Municipal, Madrid, 1981-1982.

Luna, 1982
J. J. Luna, "Nuevas apreciaciones sobre las obras de Louis-Michel van Loo en el Museo del Prado", in *Boletín del Museo del Prado*, no.9, 1982.

Luna, 1982-1983
J. J. Luna, *Luis Meléndez, bodegonista español del siglo xviii*, exh. cat., Museo del Prado, Madrid, Centro Cultural de la Caixa de Pensions, Barcelona, 1982-1983.

Luna, 1984a
J. J. Luna, "Un pequeño inventario de pinturas del Palacio de Aranjuez en torno a 1800", in *Boletín del Museo del Prado*, no. 14, 1984.

Luna, 1984b
J. J. Luna, "Miscelánea sobre bodegones de Meléndez a Goya", in *Goya*, no. 183, Madrid, 1984.

Luna, 1985a
J. J. Luna, "Nicola Vaccaro al servicio de la Corte de Madrid", in *ii Jornadas de Arte*, C. S. I. C., en Archivo Español de Arte, no. 232, 1985.

Luna, 1985b
J. J. Luna, "La peinture française en Espagne xviie et xviiie siècles", in *Revue d'Art*, 70, 1985.

Luna, 1987a
J. J. Luna, "Jean Ranc y la Corte de Felipe V en Andalucía (1730-1733)", in *Actas iii Congreso Internacional de Historia del Arte*, [Seville, 1980], en H. 16, no. 131, 1987.

Luna, 1987b
J. J. Luna, "Louis-Michel van Loo. Miscelánea pictórica" in *Urtekaria*, 1987.

Luna, 1988
J. J. Luna, "La España de Carlos III. La pintura", in *Historia 16*, 151, 1988.

Luna, 1989a
J. J. Luna, *Tesoros del Museo de Bellas Artes de Bilbao. Pintura 1400-1939*, exh. cat., Madrid, 1989.

Luna, 1989b
J. J. Luna, "Novedades y cuadros inéditos de Luis Meléndez", in *El arte en tiempos de Carlos III*, iv Jornadas de Arte, C.S.I.C., Madrid, 1989, pp. 367-376.

Luna, 1991
J. J. Luna, *Capolavori del Museo di Bellas Artes di Bilbao*, exh. cat., Padua-Rome, 1991.

Luna, 1992
J. J. Luna, *Carlos IV, mecenas de pintores y coleccionista de pinturas*, Discurso de Ingreso en la Real Academia de Doctores, Madrid, 1992.

Luna, 1993
J. J. Luna, *Las pinturas y esculturas del Palacio Real de Madrid en 1811*, Madrid, 1993.

Luna, 1994
J. J. Luna, "América en los bodegones de Luis Meléndez", in *Congreso Nacional Madrid en el contexto de lo hispánico*, Universidad Complutense, 1992, acts 1994, i, pp. 535-540.

Luna, 1995
J. J. Luna, *Los alimentos de España en la pintura: Bodegones de Luis Meléndez*, Mercasa, Madrid, 1995.

Luna, 2002-2003
J. J. Luna, 1802. *España entre dos siglos y la devolución de Menorca*, exh. cat., Mahón-Madrid, 2002-2003.

Luna, 2003
J. J. Luna, "Los frutos de las Luces", in *F. M. R.*, December, 2003, pp. 79-106.

Luna, 2004
J. J. Luna, *Guía actualizada del Museo del Prado*, [Madrid, 1984], Madrid, 2004.

Luna and Tufts, 1985
J. J. Luna and E. Tufts, *Luis Meléndez: Spanish Still Life Painter of the Eighteenth Century*, exh. cat., Raleigh-Dallas-New York, 1985.

Lynch, 1972
Lynch, *España bajo los Austrias*, Barcelona, 1972.

Madrazo, 1884
P. Madrazo, *Viaje artístico de tres siglos por las colecciones de cuadros de los Reyes de España*, Barcelona, 1884.

Mañueco Santurtún, 1997
C. Mañueco Santurtún, "Real Fábrica de Porcelana del Buen Retiro", in Fábricas de la Corona, cat. exp., Valencia-Murcia-Alicante, 1997.

Mañueco Santurtún, 1999
C. Mañueco Santurtún, "La Real Fábrica de Porcelana del Buen Retiro a través de sus documentos (1760-1808)", in *Manufactura del Buen Retiro*, exh. cat., Madrid, 1999.

Mañueco Santurtún, 2003
C. Mañueco Santurtún, *Cerámica de Alcora (1727-1827). La colección del Museo Arqueológico Nacional*, exh. cat., Talavera de la Reina, 2003.

Marañón, 1953
G. Marañón, *Nuestro siglo xviii y las Academias*, Madrid, 1953.

Marcus, 1961
F. C. Marcus, *Flower Painting by the Great Masters*, 1961.

Martín González, 1983
J. J. Martín González, *Escultura barroca en España 1600-1700*, Madrid, 1983.

Martín González, 1990
J. J. Martín González, *Luis Salvador Carmona. Escultor y académico*, Madrid, 1990.

Martínez Caviró, 1973
B. Martínez Caviró, *Porcelana del Buen Retiro. Escultura*, Madrid, 1973.

Matilla Tascón, 1960
A. Matilla Tascón, "Documentos del Archivo del Ministerio de Hacienda relativos a Pintores de Cámara y de las fábricas de Tapices y Porcelana", in *R. A. B. M.*, lxviii, 1960, p. 199.

Mayer, 1942
A. L. Mayer, *Historia de la pintura española*, Madrid, 1942.

McCoubrey, 1958
J. W. McCoubrey, *Studies in French Still Life Painting. Theory and Criticism: 1660-1860*, [Ann Arbor, Michigan], New York, 1958.

McGraw-Hill, 1970
McGraw-Hill, *Art Treasures in Spain*, New York, 1970.

Merimée, 1936
P. Merimée, *L'influence française en Espagne au xviiie siècle*, Paris, 1936.

Mesonero Romanos, 1861
R. de Mesonero Romanos, *El Antiguo Madrid*, Madrid, 1861.

Mitchell, 1973
P. Mitchell, *Great Flower Painters. Four Centuries of Floral Art*, Woodstock, New York, 1973.

Monet, 1907
D. Monet, *Le sentiment de la nature au xviiie siècle*, Paris, 1907.

Montaiglon, 1875
A. de Montaiglon, *Procés verbaux de l'Academie Royale de Peinture et de Sculpture*, Paris, 1875.

Morales Borrero, 1972
C. Morales Borrero, *Fiestas reales en el reinado de Fernando VI*, Madrid, 1972.

Morales y Marín, 1979
J. L. Morales y Marín, *Los Bayeu*, Zaragoza, 1979.

Morales y Marín, 1994
J. L. Morales y Marín, *Pintura en España (1750-1808)*, Madrid, 1994.

Morales y Marín, 1995
J. L. Morales y Marín, *Francisco Bayeu. Vida y obra*, Zaragoza, 1995.

Morales y Marín, 1996
J. L. Morales y Marín, *Mariano Salvador Maella. Vida y obra*, Zaragoza, 1996.

Morassi, 1962
A. Morassi, A *Complete Catalogue of the Paintings of G. B. Tiepolo Including Pictures by his Pupils and Followers Wrongly Atributed to him*, London, 1962.

Moulin, 1989
L. Moulin, *Les liturgies de la table*, Amberes, 1989.

Mousnier, Labrousse and Bouloiseau, 1953
R. Mousnier, E. Labrousse and M. Bouloiseau, *Le xviiieme siècle: Révolution intelectuelle, technique et politique (1715-1815)*, Paris, 1953.

Nard, 1859
F. Nard, *Guía de Aranjuez*, Madrid, 1859.

Newsweek, 1968
Newsweek, *Prado. Madrid*, New York, 1968.

Oliveras Guart, 1973
A. Oliveras Guart, *Real Sitio de Aranjuez*, Madrid, 1973.

Onieva, 1956
A. Onieva, *La pintura española en el Prado*, Madrid, 1956.

Opperman, 1977
H. Opperman, *Jean-Baptiste Oudry*, New York-London, 1977.

Orellana, 1967
M. A. Orellana, *Biografía pictórica valenciana*, ed. X. de Salas, Valencia, 1967.

Orozco Díaz, 1947
E. Orozco Díaz, *Temas del Barroco*, Granada, 1947.

Ossorio y Bernard, 1883-1884
M. Ossorio y Bernard, *Galería biográfica de artistas españoles del siglo xix*, Madrid, 1883-1884.

Otero Túñez, 1980
R. Otero Túñez, *El Barroco y el Rococó. La escultura*, Madrid, 1980.

Pacheco, 1990
F. Pacheco, *Arte de la pintura*, [Seville, 1649] [ed. Sánchez Cantón, 1956], ed. Bassegoda, 1990.

Pallucchini, 1968
A. Pallucchini, *L'opera completa di Gian Battista Tiepolo*, Milan, 1968.

Palomino y Velasco, 1947
A. A. Palomino y Velasco, *Museo pictórico y escala óptica con el Parnaso español pintoresco y laureado*, [Madrid, 1715-1724], Madrid, 1947.

Parslow, 1998
C. Parslow, *Rediscovering Antiquity*, Cambridge, 1998.

Paviere, 1963
S. Paviere, *A Dictionary of Flower, Fruit and Still Life Painters*, Leigh-on-Sea, 1963.

Pedrocco, 2002
F. Pedrocco, *Giambattista Tiepolo*, Milan-París, 2002.

Pemán, 1930
C. Pemán, *El arte en Cádiz*, Madrid, 1930.

Peñasco y Cambronero, 1990
H. Peñasco y C. Cambronero, *Las calles de Madrid*, [1860 (?)], facimile ed., Madrid, 1990.

Perera, 1958
R. Perera, "Carlos IV. Mecenas y coleccionista de obras de arte", in *Archivo Español*, 1958, p. 12.

Pérez Guillén, 1991
I. V. Pérez Guillén, *La pintura cerámica valenciana del siglo xviii*, Valencia, 1991.

Pérez Sánchez, 1965
A. E. Pérez Sánchez, *Pintura italiana del siglo xvii en España*, Madrid, 1965.

Pérez Sánchez, 1967
A. E. Pérez Sánchez, "Sobre bodegones italianos, napolitanos especialmente", in *Archivo Español de Arte*, 1967, p. 309.

Pérez Sánchez, 1972
A. E. Pérez Sánchez, "Notas sobre Palomino pintor", in *Archivo Español de Arte*, 1972, p. 251.

Pérez Sánchez, 1974
A. E. Pérez Sánchez, *El Museo del Prado*, Madrid, 1974.

Pérez Sánchez, 1982
A. E. Pérez Sánchez, *La Academia madrileña de 1603 y sus fundadores*, Valladolid, 1982.

Pérez Sánchez, 1983-1984
A. E. Pérez Sánchez, *Pintura española de bodegones y floreros de 1600 a Goya*, exh. cat., Museo del Prado, Madrid, 1983-1984.

Pérez Sánchez, 1987
A. E. Pérez Sánchez, *La nature morte espagnole du xviie siècle à Goya*, Office du Livre, Freiburg, 1987.

Pérez Sánchez, 1988
A. E. Pérez Sánchez, *Pintura barroca en España (1600-1750)*, Madrid, 1988.

Pérez Vidal, 1958
Pérez Vidal, *Catálogo de la colección de cucharas de madera y de asta*, Dirección General de Bellas Artes, Madrid, 1958.

Pignatti, 1966
T. Pignatti, *La pittura del Settecento in Inghilterra e in Spagna*, Milan, 1966.

Pillsbury, Jordan and Cummings, 1985
E. Pillsbury, W. Jordan and P Cummings, *In Pursuit of Quality*. The Kimbell Museum, Fort Worth, 1985.

Pitsch, 1949
M. Pitsch, *La vie populaire au xviiie siècle d'après les textes et des estampes*, Paris, 1949.

Plaza, 1975
F. J. de la Plaza, *El Palacio Real Nuevo de Madrid*, Valladolid, 1975.

Plaza Prieto, 1976
J. Plaza Prieto, *Estructura económica de España en el siglo xviii*, Madrid, 1976.

Pleguezuelo, 2000
A. Pleguezuelo, "Cerámicas para agua en el barroco español", in *Cuadernos de Arte*, Universitat de Valencia, Valencia, 2000.

Plinio, 1984
Plinio el Viejo, *Historia natural*, London, 1984.

Pluche, 1732
N. A. Pluche, *Spectacle de la Nature*, Paris, 1732.

Ponz, 1947
A. Ponz, Viaje de *España*, [Madrid, 1772-1794], Madrid, 1947.

Pothiades, 1963
W. Pothiades, *Eighteenth Century Painting*, New York, 1963.

Pradillo, 1997
J. M. Pradillo, *Alfareros toledanos*, Toledo, 1997.

Préclin, 1952
E. Préclin, *Le xviiieme siècle*, Paris, 1952.

Prota-Giurleo, 1953
U. Prota-Giurleo, *Pittori napoletani del Seicento*, Naples, 1953.

Puerto Sarmiento, 1988
F. J. Puerto Sarmiento, "Botánica, medicina terapéutica y jardines botánicos", in *Madrid*, 1988, pp. 295-306.

Ramírez Montesinos, 1996
E Ramírez Montesinos, "Cristales", in *La vida cotidiana en tiempos de Goya*, exh. cat. [organised by Natacha Seseña], Museo Arqueológico, Madrid, 1996, pp. 177-180.

Réau, 1971
L. Réau, *L'Europe française au siècle des lumières*, Paris, 1971.

Rincón García, 1988
W. Rincón García, "Iconografía de la real y distinguida orden de Carlos III", *Fragmentos*, nos. 12-13-14, 1988, pp. 144-161.

Rius Oliva, 1964
S. Rius Oliva, "Los hermanos González Velázquez pintores del siglo xviii", in *Revista de la Universidad de Madrid*, no. 52, 1964.

Rocamora, 1972
M. Rocamora, *Breves datos biográficos del pintor Luis Meléndez (1716-1780)*, Barcelona, 1972.

Rodríguez Gutiérrez de Ceballos, 1971
A. Rodríguez Gutiérrez de Ceballos,
Los Churriguera, Madrid, 1971.

Rodríguez Gutiérrez de Ceballos, 1992
A. Rodríguez Gutiérrez de Ceballos,
*El siglo xviii. Entre tradición y
academia*, Madrid, 1992.

Roettgen, 1999
S. Roettgen, *Anton Raphael Mengs
1728-1779. Das malerische und
zeichnerische werk*, Munich, 1999.

Roland-Michel, 1978
M. Roland-Michel, *Anne Vallayer-
Coster, 1774-1818*, Paris, 1978.

**Rose de Viejo, Parra and Jiménez-López,
2001**
I. Rose de Viejo, E. la Parra and E.
Jiménez-López, *La imagen de
Manuel Godoy*, Junta de
Extremadura, Mérida, 2001.

Rose Wagner, 1983
I. Rose Wagner, *Manuel Godoy:
patrón de las artes y coleccionista*,
2 vols., Universidad Complutense
de Madrid, 1983.

Rosenberg, Slive and Ter Kuile, 1977
J. Rosenberg, S. Slive and E. H.
Ter Kuile, *Dutch Art 1600-1800*,
Harmondsworth, 1977.

Rosenberg, 1963
P. Rosenberg, *Chardin*, Geneva,
1963.

Rouches, 1927
G. Rouches, "Le portrait de Louis
Meléndez par lui-même", in *R. A. A.
M.*, 1927, p. 248.

Ruiz Alcón, 1969
M. T. Ruiz Alcón, *Vidrio y cristal de
La Granja*, Madrid, 1969.

Salas, 1977
X. de Salas, "Inéditos de Luis Paret y
otras notas sobre él mismo", in
Archivo Español de Arte, no. 199,
1977.

Salas y Águeda, 1980
X. de Salas y M. Águeda, *Antón
Rafael Mengs*, exh. cat., Museo del
Prado, Madrid, 1980.

Sambricio, 1946
V. Sambricio, *Los tapices de Goya*,
Madrid, 1946.

Sambricio, 1955
V. Sambricio, *Francisco Bayeu*,
Madrid, 1955.

Sambricio, 1958
V. Sambricio, *José del Castillo*,
Madrid, 1958.

Sánchez Cantón, 1916
F. J. Sánchez Cantón, "Los pintores
de Cámara de los reyes de España",
in *Boletín de la Sociedad Española de
Excursiones*, 1916.

Sánchez Cantón, 1929
F. J. Sánchez Cantón, "El
Autorretrato de Luis Meléndez en el
Museo del Louvre", in *Archivo
Español de Arte*, 1929.

Sánchez Cantón, 1931-1943
F. J. Sánchez Cantón, *Fuentes
literarias para la historia del arte
español*, Madrid, 1931-1943.

Sánchez Cantón, 1952
F. J. Sánchez Cantón, "Los
antecedentes, la fundación y la
historia de la Real Academia de
Bellas Artes", in *Academia*, 1952.

Sánchez Cantón, 1959-1960
F. J. Sánchez Cantón, "Las Bellas
Artes en el reinado de Fernando VI",
in *Academia*, 1959-1960.

Sánchez Cantón, 1962
F. J. Sánchez Cantón, *Tesoros de la
pintura en el Prado*, Madrid, 1962.

Sánchez Cantón, 1965
F. J. Sánchez Cantón, *Escultura y
pintura del siglo xviii. Francisco de
Goya*, Ars Hispaniae, vol. xvii,
Madrid, 1965.

Sánchez Cantón, 1966
F. J. Sánchez Cantón, *The Prado*,
Thames and Hudson, London, 1966.

Sánchez de Palacios, 1965
M. Sánchez de Palacios, *Bodegones
en el Museo del Prado*, Madrid, 1965.

Santamaría Arnáiz, 1989
M. Santamaría Arnáiz, "La
alimentación", in *La vida cotidiana
en la España de Velázquez*, Madrid,
1989.

Santiago Páez, 1966
E. M. Santiago Páez, "El pintor
Miguel Jacinto Meléndez", in
*Revista de Archivos, Bibliotecas y
Museos*, 1966.

Santiago Páez, 1989
E. M. Santiago Páez, *Miguel Jacinto
Meléndez, pintor de Felipe V*,
Oviedo, 1989.

Santiago Páez, 1989-1990
E. M. Santiago Páez, *Miguel Jacinto
Meléndez, pintor de Felipe V*, Museo
de Bellas Artes de Asturias, Oviedo,
Museo Municipal, Madrid,
1989-1990.

Sarrailh, 1974
J. Sarrailh, *La España ilustrada
de la segunda mitad del siglo xviii*,
Madrid, 1974.

Saule, 1996
B. Saule, *Versailles triomphant. Une
journée de Louis XIV*, Paris, 1996.

Schneider, 1992
N. Schneider, *Naturaleza muerta*,
Cologne, 1992.

Segal, 1982
S. Segal, *A Flowery Past*, exh. cat.,
Amsterdam, 1982.

Sentenach, 1907
N. Sentenach, *La pintura en Madrid
desde sus orígenes hasta el siglo xix*,
Madrid, 1907.

Serdio, 2003
E. de Serdio, *Del vidrio y la botella
de vino*, Madrid, 2003.

Serullaz, 1947
M. Serullaz, *Evolution de la peinture
espagnole*, Paris, 1947.

Seseña, 1975
N. Seseña, *Cerámica popular en
Castilla la Nueva*, Madrid, 1975.

Seseña, 1984
N. Seseña, "Lozas castellanas,
bodegones, coleccionistas", in
*Cerámica de Talavera de la Reina y
Puente del Arzobispo*, Col. Bertrán
y Musitu, exh. cat., Museo de
Cerámica y Artes Decorativas,
Barcelona, 1984.

Seseña, 1989
N. Seseña, *Las lozas de Talavera y
Puente*, exh. cat., Madrid,
1989.

Seseña, 1991
N. Seseña, "El búcaro de las
Meninas", in *Archivo Español de
Arte*, CSIC, Madrid, 1991.

Seseña, 1996
N. Seseña, *La vida cotidiana en
tiempos de Goya*, exh. cat., Museo
Arqueológico, Madrid, 1996.

Seseña, 1997
N. Seseña, *Cacharrería popular.
La alfarería de basto en España*,
Madrid, 1997.

Seseña, 2000
N. Seseña, *El rango de la cerámica en
el bodegón*, Galaxia Gutenberg,
Madrid, 2000.

Seseña, 2003 [in print]
N. Seseña, *Goya y las mujeres*,
Madrid, 2003 [in print].

Sestieri, 2000
G. Sestieri, *Nature morte italiane ed
europee del xvii e xviii secolo*, exh.
cat., Rome, 2000.

Soria, 1948
M. Soria, "Firmas de Luis Egidio
Meléndez", in *Archivo Español de
Arte*, vol. 21, no. 83, 1948.

Spinosa, 1971
N. Spinosa, *La pittura napolitana da
Carlo a Ferdinando IV di Borbone*,
Storia di Napoli VIII, Naples, 1971.

Spinosa, 1979
N. Spinosa, *Le arte figurative a
Napoli nel Settecento. Documenti e
ricerche*, Naples, 1979.

Spike, 1983
J. T. Spike, *Italian Still Life Paintings from Three Centuries*, exh. cat., New York-Tulsa-Dayton, 1983.

Sterling, 1952
C. Sterling, *La Nature Morte de l'Antiquité à nos Jours*, Paris, 1952.

Sterling, 1981
C. Sterling, *Still Life Painting: From Antiquity to the Twentieth Century*, New York, 1981.

Subias Galter, 1951
J. Subias Galter, *Un siglo olvidado de pintura catalana*, Barcelona, 1951.

Sullivan, 1982
E. J. Sullivan, *Goya and the Art of his Time*, exh. cat., Dallas, 1982.

Symmons, 1988
S. Symmons, *Goya, In Pursuit of Patronage*, London, 1988.

Taxonera, 1943
Taxonera, *Isabel de Farnesio. Retrato de una reina y perfil de una mujer (1692-1766)*, Barcelona, 1943.

Thieme-Becker, 1907-1950
Thieme-Becker, *Allgemeines Lexikon der Bildenden Künstler*, Leipzig, 1907-1950.

Thuillier y Chatelet, 1964
J. Thuillier and A. Chatelet, *La pintura francesa de Le Nain à Fragonard*, Geneva-Barcelona, 1964.

Tissot, 1982
A. Tissot, *Voyage de Pierre Jacquet-Droz à la cour du Roi D'Espagne 1758-1759 d'aprés le journal d'Abraham Louis Sandoz, son beau-père*, Neuchâtel, 1982.

Tomlinson, 1989
J. Tomlinson, *Graphic Evolutions: The Prints Series of Francisco de Goya*, New York, 1989.

Tomlinson, 1990
J. Tomlinson, "The provenance and patronage of Luis Meléndez's Aranjuez still lifes", in *The Burlington Magazine*, 1043, 1990, pp. 84-89.

Tormo, 1932
E. Tormo, *Aranjuez*, Madrid, 1932.

Torres Martín, 1971
R. Torres Martín, *La naturaleza muerta en la pintura española*, Barcelona, 1971.

Tortella, 1996
T. Tortella, en Natacha Seseña, *La vida cotidiana en tiempos de Goya*, exh. cat., Museo Arqueológico, Madrid, 1996.

Tovar Martín, 1979
V. Tovar Martín, *La arquitectura olvidada madrileña de la primera mitad del siglo xviii*, Madrid, 1979.

Triado, 1975
J. R. Triado, "Juan van der Hamen, bodegonista", in *Estudios Pro Arte*, no. 1, 1975.

Trujillo, 1981
C. Trujillo, "Juan García de Miranda. Dos series de sus lienzos en el Museo del Prado", in *Boletín del Museo del Prado*, no. 4, 1981, p. 11.

Tufts, 1971
E. Tufts, *A Stylistic Study of the Paintings of Luis Meléndez*, New York University, New York, 1971.

Tufts, 1972
E. Tufts, "Luis Meléndez. Documents on his life and work", in *Art Bulletin*, 1972.

Tufts, 1974
E. Tufts, "A Second Meléndez Self-Portrait: the Artist as Still Life", in *A. B.*, 1974.

Tufts, 1977
E. Tufts, "The Veristic Eye: Some Contemporary American Affinities with Luis Meléndez, Spanish Painter of Still Life Phenomenology", in *Arts Magazine*, no. 52, December 1977.

Tufts, 1982
E. Tufts, "Luis Meléndez, Still Life painter sans pareil", in *Gazette des Beaux-Arts*, November 1982.

Tufts, 1985a
E. Tufts, *Luis Meléndez: Eighteenth Century Master of the Spanish Still Life with a Catalogue Raisonne*, University of Missouri Press, Columbia, 1985.

Tufts, 1985b
E. Tufts, *Luis Meléndez: Spanish Still Life Painter of the Eighteenth Century*, exh. cat., Meadows Museum, Southern Methodist University, Dallas, 1985.

Úbeda de los Cobos, 1988
A. Úbeda de los Cobos, *Mentalidad e ideología en la Real Academia de Bellas Artes de San Fernando, 1741-1800*, 2 vols., Universidad Complutense de Madrid, 1988.

Urrea Fernández, 1973
J. Urrea Fernández, "Juan Bautista Peña y Pablo Pernicharo, pintores españoles del siglo xviii", in *R. U. C.*, xxii, 1973.

Urrea Fernández, 1977
J. Urrea Fernández, *Pintura italiana del siglo xviii en España*, Valladolid, 1977.

Urrea Fernández, 1979-1981
J. Urrea Fernández, "Introducción a la pintura rococó en España", in *Coloquio La época de Fernando VI*, Oviedo, 1979-1981.

Valdivieso, 1986
E. Valdivieso, *Historia de la pintura sevillana. Siglos xiii al xx*, Seville, 1986.

Valdivieso and Serrera, 1982
E. Valdivieso and J. M. Serrera, *La época de Murillo. Antecedentes y consecuencias de su pintura*, Seville, 1982.

Vega, 1980
A. Vega, *Insanno e Realtá. Trompe l'oeil in Europa xvi-xvii*, Bergamo, 1980.

Warner, 1975
R. Warner, *Dutch and Flemish Fruit and Flower Painters of 17th and 18th Centuries*, [Amsterdam, 1928] 2nd ed. 1975.

Waterhouse, 1969
E. Waterhouse, *Italian Baroque Painting*, London, 1969.

Waterhouse, 1976
E. Waterhouse, *Roman Baroque Painting*, Oxford, 1976.

Weisberg and Talbot, 1979
P. Weisberg and W. S. Talbot, *Chardin and the Still Life, Tradition in France*, Cleveland, 1979.

Whistler, 1986
C. Whistler, "G. B. Tiepolo at the Court of Charles III", in *The Burlington Magazine*, 128, 1986.

Wiesenthal, 1979
M. Wiesenthal, *Treasures of Spanish Painting*, New York, 1979.

Wildenstein, 1963
G. Wildenstein, *J. B. S. Chardin*, Zurich, 1963.

Wittkower, 1963
R. and M. Wittkower, *Born Under Saturn*, New York, 1963.

Wittkower, 1973
R. Wittkower, *Art and Architecture in Italy (1600-1750)*, Baltimore, 1973.

Wittkower, 1979
R. Wittkower, *Art and Architecture in Italy (1600-1750)*, [London, 1958], Madrid, 1979.

Young, 1976
E. Young, "New Perspectives on Spanish Still Life Paintings of the Golden Age", in *The Burlington Magazine*, 118, 1976, p. 203.

Zarco Cuevas, 1934
J. Zarco Cuevas, *Cuadros reunidos por Carlos IV siendo Príncipe, en su Casa de Campo de El Escorial*, El Escorial, 1934.

List of exhibitions

Berlin, 1982
Mythen der Neuen Welt, Martin Gropius Bas, Berlin, 1982.

Bilbao, 1991-1992
Luis Paret y Alcázar (1746-1799), by Javier González de Durana and Juan J. Luna, Museo de Bellas Artes, Bilbao, 1991-1992.

Bilbao, 1999-2000
El bodegón español de Zurbarán a Picasso, by Francisco Calvo Serraller *et al.*, Museo de Bellas Artes, 1999-2000.

Bordeaux, 1978
La nature morte de Brueghel à Soutine, Musée des Beaux-Arts, Bordeaux, 1978.

Bordeaux-Paris-Madrid, 1979-1980
El arte europeo en la Corte de España durante el siglo xviii, Musée des Beaux-Arts, Bordeaux, Grand Palais, Paris, Museo del Prado, Madrid, 1979-1980.

Caracas, 1981
400 años de pintura española, Museo de Bellas Artes, Caracas, 1981.

El Escorial, 1986
Las Casas Reales. El Palacio, Monasterio de San Lorenzo de El Escorial, 1986.

Stockholm, 1959-1960
Stora Spanska Mastare, Nationalmuseum, Stockholm, 1959-1960.

Stockholm, 1995
Stilleben, Nationalmuseum, Stockholm, 1995

Florence, 1986
Da El Greco a Goya. Il Secolo d'Oro della Pittura Espagnola, Sala d'Arme di Palazzo Vecchio, Florence, 1986.

Florence, 2003
La natura morta italiana da Caravaggio al Settecento, by Mina Gregori *et al.*, Palazzo Strozzi, Florence, 2003.

Frankfurt, 1999-2000
Mehr Licht. Europa um 1770. Die bilden de Kunst der Aufklarüng, Städelches Kunstinstitut und Städische Galerie, Frankfurt, 1999-2000.

Geneva, 1989
Du Greco à Goya: chefs d'oeuvre du Prado et des collections espagnoles, Musée d'Art et d'Histoire, Geneva, 1989.

Indianapolis, 1997
Painting in Spain in the Age of Enlightenment. Goya and His Contemporaries, by Ronda Kasl, Suzanne Stratton *et al.*, Museum of Art, Indianapolis, 1997.

Jackson, 2001
The Majesty of Spain, Mississippi Arts Pavilion, Jackson, 2001.

La Granja de San Ildefonso, 2000
El Real Sitio de La Granja de San Ildefonso. Retrato y escena del rey, by Delfín Rodríguez *et al.*, La Granja de San Ildefonso, 2000.

Las Palmas de Gran Canaria, 1973
Pintura española de los siglos xvi al xix, Casa de Colón, Las Palmas de Gran Canaria, 1973.

London, 1954-1955
European Masters of the Eighteenth Century, Royal Academy, London, 1954-1955.

London, 1972
The Age of Neoclassicism, Royal Academy, London, 1972.

London, 1986-1987
Director's Choice: Selected Acquisitions 1973-86, National Gallery, London, 1986-1987.

London, 1989
Painting in Spain during the Later Eighteenth Century, by Michael Helston, National Gallery, London, 1989.

London, 1995
Spanish Still Life from Velázquez to Goya, by William B. Jordan and Peter Cherry, National Gallery, London, 1995.

London 1997
An Eye on Nature. Spanish Still Life Paintings from Sánchez Cotán to Goya, by William B. Jordan, Matthiesen Fine Art Ltd., London, 1997.

Lyons, 1982
Fleurs de Lyon 1807-1917, Musée des Beaux-Arts, Lyons, 1982.

Madrid, 1936-1940
Floreros y bodegones en la pintura española, by Julio Cavestany, Palacio de la Biblioteca Nacional, Madrid, 1936-1940.

Madrid, 1950
Exposición de Oleicultura, Ministerio de Agricultura, Madrid, 1950.

Madrid, 1983-1984
Pintura española de bodegones y floreros de 1600 a Goya, by Alfonso E. Pérez Sánchez, Museo del Prado, Madrid, 1983-1984.

Madrid, 1987
Tesoros de las colecciones particulares madrileñas, Comunidad de Madrid, Madrid, 1987.

Madrid, 1988-1989
Carlos III y la Ilustración, Palacio de Velázquez, Madrid, 1988-1989.

Madrid, 1989-1990
Tesoros del Museo de Bellas Artes de Bilbao. Pintura 1400-1939, by Juan J. Luna, Museo Municipal, Madrid, 1989-1990.

Madrid, 1990-1991
Miguel Jacinto Meléndez (1679-1734), by E. M. Santiago Páez, Museo Municipal, Madrid, 1990-1991.

Madrid, 1995
La belleza de lo real. Floreros y bodegones españoles en el Museo del Prado 1600-1800, by Trinidad de Antonio *et al.*, Museo del Prado, Madrid, 1995.

Madrid, 1995-1996
Goya en las colecciones españolas, BBV, Madrid, 1995-1996.

Madrid, 1996
Goya. 250 aniversario, Museo Nacional del Prado, Madrid, 1996.

Madrid, 1997
Los cinco sentidos y el arte, Museo del Prado, Madrid, 1997.

Madrid, 2000
El documento pintado, Museo del Prado, Madrid, 2000.